Convert Every Click

Make More Money Online with Holistic Conversion Rate Optimization

Benji Rabhan

WILEY

Cover image: Paul McCarthy
Cover design: iStockphoto.com (Mouse: © Materio/Money: © DNY59)

Published by John Wiley & Sons, Inc., Hoboken, New Jersey.
Published simultaneously in Canada.

For general information about our other products and services, please contact our Customer Care
Department within the United States at (800) 762-2974, outside the United States at (317) 572-3993
or fax (317) 572-4002.

Wiley publishes in a variety of print and electronic formats and by print-on-demand. Some material
included with standard print versions of this book may not be included in e-books or in print-on-
demand. If this book refers to media such as a CD or DVD that is not included in the version you
purchased, you may download this material at http://booksupport.wiley.com. For more information
about Wiley products, visit www.wiley.com.

ISBN: 978-1-118-75967-7 (cloth); ISBN 978-1-118-75974-5 (ebk); ISBN 978-1-118-75970-7 (ebk)

Printed in the United States of America

10 9 8 7 6 5 4 3 2 1

For Jenna,

thanks for putting up with my many long hours during the writing of this book.

For my parents, Joe and Bebe,

thank you for being early adopters and buying that first computer.

And Dad, thanks for making me try new things, even when I didn't want to.

CONTENTS

ACKNOWLEDGMENTS

I'd like to thank Julie, Pat, Kevin, Adrianna, Brian, Lauren, Susan, Josh, and the rest of my team members for helping with this book.

PREFACE

Think about all the clicks on your web pages, on your e-mail, on your banner ads, on your social media posts, on all your online marketing. Now imagine each one of those clicks converted into cash in your pocket. Sounds pretty cool, doesn't it? It might also sound like an impossible dream, or some hyped-up sales pitch. But it's not; "converting every click" is what companies that do business online can strive for. Can you truly convert every single click into cash? Let's think about it for a moment. If we give each person who comes in contact with your company exactly what they want, exactly how they want it, exactly when they want it—then, theoretically, they should buy. In other words, if we give each person an individualized experience that's customized to their wants, needs, and preferences, then theoretically they should always choose to buy from you. This might sound like a practical impossibility; but in theory, the idea is sound. When you combine the data gathering and testing technology that currently exists with a strong knowledge of psychology and human behavior, you can move closer and closer to customizing experiences for the individual. That brings you closer and closer to the goal of converting every click.

But is this really possible? Let's look at how far we've come in a relatively short time. First there was the Internet. And it was good. Smart businesses put up websites, mostly ugly ones, but any website was good enough. These were the early days of Web 1.0 when the Internet was basically a collection of online brochures. Websites were almost exclusively company-centric or creator-centric. Everything on the site revolved around what that company or creator wanted to say. In fact, the term *brochure website* was coined to mean a company-centric informational site.

Over time, technology and people's comfort with interacting online led to a desire for users to interact with their online experience a little. The dawn of Web 2.0 saw user-generated content, such as blog commenting, product reviews, and eventually more sophisticated social media websites. Although this era gave users the ability to contribute to the web experience, the site owners were primarily delivering information and one-size-fits-all content. In fact, most of the web still operates this way.

Right now, we're entering a new age of the customer-centric web. I like to call it Web 3.0. It's an age of a learning web, where websites are customized for the individual user as much as possible. Every experience is unique to the user. The websites actually change based on who is looking at them.

Think about it for a moment, and you'll see this is already happening. Google uses data it knows about you, such as where you're located, your preferences, what you're searching for, and other factors, to make a customized experience that's more relevant to you. Amazon does something similar by offering individual recommendations for you based on what you've searched for in the past, what you've bought in the past, and other related metrics. Every Facebook News Feed is completely unique, based on you, your friends, and your preferences.

It may sound scary to people when they learn how much data can be collected and how a website can be altered to appeal to them individually. It all sounds a bit Big Brother to many people. However, the world is heading this way whether we like it or not. If your company (or the company you work for) doesn't adapt to this new age centered on the individual user, you won't be on the cutting edge. And you risk falling behind competitors.

Until recently, leveraging the power of the customer-centric web was only truly accessible to huge corporations like Google, Amazon, and Facebook. But even these companies now allow advertisers to reach users using similar data to target people that their products or services are the most relevant to. Web 3.0 is here, and the technology gives businesses the power to use data to come closer to converting every click into a lead or a customer. For example, as a Facebook advertiser, you can target users down to an extremely granular level.

Businesses are finally figuring out they need a combination of things to be successful online. They need a professional-looking website. They need traffic, preferably from a wide variety of sources, and they need results that help them make money. These results are what we broadly call conversion. At the end of the day, businesses need to convert the traffic coming to their website into money.

The goals are no different in the off-line world of brick-and-mortar businesses. Whether you operate a bank, a bakery, a clothing boutique, or whatever—the goal is to turn casual browsers into customers. You do that by making the shopping experience easy and enjoyable. You put signs in the right places, make up displays to attract the eye, suggest accessories and add-ons, and make sure the pathways direct people where you want them to go. However, even though you're optimizing the experience to make more sales, each person who walks in the door will get the same experience.

Because the online world is digital, you can theoretically customize the experience to the individual user. If one person doesn't qualify to use a certain product line, that person doesn't even need to see that section of your website. You can further customize your online storefront so that it advertises items in many different ways, depending on who's looking at it. The more you customize your marketing for the individual, the higher your conversions will be. Changing the experience for every individual customer was just not feasible before the Internet.

But it is feasible today. Even now, the overwhelming majority of online businesses have no idea how much money they're leaving on the table by not moving toward a more customer-centric experience.

It's no longer good enough to have a pretty website or loads of traffic. Whether you run an Internet-based company or a brick-and-mortar store trying to boost sales with a website, for your business to survive online, you must be able to convert those anonymous browsers into buyers. But where do you start?

Well, most people start by taking a stab in the dark. They hire a web designer to build a website. They tell the developer what they want, but what they want isn't necessarily what they *need*. What they want is usually a beautiful site. What they need goes beyond beauty and incorporates systems and functions that convert visitors to customers.

If things don't go as well as they hoped, they start making random changes all over the place, hoping something will help boost their profits. If they're unsure what to do, they might change the entire website or redo their branding. If they're a little more experienced with online marketing, they might rewrite their sales scripts or pour more money into advertising. Sometimes these things help; sometimes they make matters worse. The big problem is they aren't making changes *scientifically*. They're going about it randomly and not tracking the results correctly—or at all.

A better, safer way to go about turning more browsers into buyers (or anonymous visitors into qualified leads) is using what are known as conversion rate optimization techniques to lead you toward a higher converting website. Traditionally, conversion rate optimization is the science of tweaking and improving a website to convert the maximum number of people possible into paying customers or leads.

You may have heard that unless you are converting at 100 percent (meaning "converting every click" as the title of this book suggests), there's always room for improvement. Hopefully you realize that's like the expression *reaching for the moon*. You don't literally mean to reach for the moon, your arms are too short. Unfortunately, many people do take it too literally, and it sends them into too granular a direction for too long.

Sometimes it might be better for your company if you go back to the drawing board for that page you've been working on, or maybe turn your focus to another step in the sales process. I do this a lot with my clients because our goal is to put their time and money where it's going to give them the best return on their investment.

Let's get a little perspective. Say a hypothetical sales website has a conversion rate of around 1 to 2 percent. That might be pretty good for that industry, but that means 98 percent of browsers on the site are not converting. In theory, that means there's a lot of potential revenue going down the drain. One solution is to pour more money into traffic generation, which is a common Internet marketing practice. Get more people, you make more money, even with a 1 percent conversion rate, right?

But what if you could lift that rate to 3 or 4 percent without increasing your budget? Suddenly, you're making way more money from your existing traffic. Regardless of your actual current conversion rates, even a tiny lift in overall conversions can mean huge improvements to your bottom line. You didn't have to buy more advertising. You just needed to make the right tweaks. Now, conversion rates don't always transfer directly to your bottom line. For now, just realize that you can work with what you've got, make improvements, and wind up with more money at the end of the day.

Conversion rate optimization is becoming a new buzzword in online marketing for a good reason. More and more people are looking for ways to maximize the sales and number of leads they get from the visitors coming to their websites. The sooner you start optimizing your conversions, the better.

For the past decade and a half, the Internet has been like the Wild West—a gold mine for those who figured it out, largely free and unregulated. Things have evolved a lot since then. Web traffic is becoming more and more competitive to buy, and it will only continue to move in that direction. Free traffic is also getting more competitive and, therefore, less free.

The best way to stand out and thrive online, now and in the future, is to make the most out of every ounce of traffic you get. Every visitor, every click, and every lead should be measured and cataloged, and a relationship should be established with as many of those leads as possible. Once you know a lot about your visitors, you can focus your efforts on creating a customer-centric environment where more of them will convert.

Don't worry if you've gotten to this point and have no idea what your conversion rate is. It's a much more complex metric than commonly thought. Whatever your conversion rate is now, conversion rate optimization will take you to the next level in your profit margin. Demand for information on the topic of conversion rate optimization is growing. It's a specialized skill set that is rarely taught anywhere online or in the academic world because it's still fairly new (from an academic perspective, at least). Conversion rate optimization used to be available only to large companies who could afford to pay consultants a fair, but sizeable, fee, as well as building or buying the infrastructure they needed. That's always bothered me a little. It feels ironic to say that because I am one of those consultants, but I can't serve everyone. So this book is my way of helping you understand what your visitors are doing and helping you get the most out of your website by leading you toward converting every click using conversion rate optimization. With conversion rate optimization, companies can experience significant growth without added expense.

In the end, when you combine the power of conversion rate optimization and the customer-centric web, everyone wins. It's the best of both worlds—the user gets the best experience, and the company gets the best conversion rates.

Let's dive in, shall we?

How to Get the Most out of This Book

This book is designed to be more than just a collection of concepts and abstract ideas. I want you to be able to really use what you learn to grow your business in a meaningful way.

Each chapter will introduce the strategies, techniques, and psychology behind my particular methodology of improving your conversions. Although I will sneak in specific ideas that will help you, my goal with this book is not to give you many hard-and-fast rules because I don't believe that's how conversion rate optimization works. Every business is different and every viewer is unique, so hard-and-fast rules and best practices just don't apply often enough.

If I told you that an orange button will convert better than a blue button or a two-column format will convert better than a magazine layout, I would absolutely be wrong—at least *sometimes*. As you're going to learn, I see things from a different perspective than most conversion rate optimization consultants out there. Every business is unique, and every set of circumstances is different. What works for one site may not work for another site. It's extremely rare to find any conversion rate optimization idea that works on every website. You're going to learn how to split test to get real results based on actual improvements to *your* site, not theories based on someone else's data.

I want you to learn the underlying reasons and psychology behind *why* certain techniques work better than others for improving conversions. So you'll hear me talking about what I call Universal Conversion Logic rather than so-called best practices. Once you have an understanding of the foundations and how they play a role in your conversion rates, you can come up with endless ideas, and your success rate will be better.

Speaking of success rates, don't worry if your ideas don't result in higher conversion rates every time. That's normal, and it's why we test the ideas to make sure we only implement the winners. In the conversion rate industry, it's often said if 4 out of 10 of your split test ideas win, you're doing well. When I heard that for the first time, I had already been consulting for a couple of years, and I didn't realize that most conversion companies had such a low success rate. Our success rates (based on the principles in this book) resulted in an average success rate of over 8 out of 10, meaning 8 out of 10 tests we ran resulted in a success—a higher conversion rate for our clients.

Build Your Skills

Some of the concepts introduced in a chapter will need some practice for you to get good at implementing them in your own business. Also, we can fit only so much information in this book. So I've set up a special skills lab on our website where you can practice what you've learned in a safe environment. You can sign up for a free account right now by going to www.ConvertEveryClick.com/skillslab. You'll build your confidence and be able to take the concept from the abstract to practical use. Any time we have a skills lab set up for a chapter, you'll be shown exactly where to find it online in the Build Your Skills section at the end of each chapter.

Finally, I want to make a quick note about the examples in this book. Whenever possible, I will try to offer real-world illustrations of the concepts we're discussing. It's important to know that these are tested and proven strategies, not just theories. Unfortunately, because of the confidential nature of the relationship I have with my clients (especially the larger ones), I had to be careful about what I could share. Fortunately, I was able to use many examples from companies I own without having to be concerned about confidentiality.

I know from experience that most people learn better when they try things for themselves. So while I do my best to include good examples through the book, I strongly encourage you to take notes and jot down ideas as you go. Remember, you'll never know how powerful an idea can be if you forget it. And you'll never know for sure if it's a powerful idea until you test it. (We'll talk about that more later.)

CHAPTER ONE

What Is Holistic Conversion Rate Optimization?

When talking about conversion rate optimization, we often talk about low-hanging fruit in reference to ideas that easily and/or quickly improve conversions. Who wouldn't want some low-hanging fruit? Easy pickings are often where we find some of the fastest and highest returns.

When I look at the idea of low-hanging fruit, a whole series of questions comes to my mind. What is low-hanging fruit? What makes one fruit a better pick than another? Can you tell if a conversion idea is ripe just by looking at it? If you have to start cutting branches, which branch is best? And when you get right down to it, isn't all fruit low-hanging if you cut down the tree?

Let me be clear, I am not suggesting you cut down your marketing tree because then the tree will die. I am also not necessarily suggesting that you have to start over with your website to improve conversions. The secret to why a fruit hangs low on a tree is often embedded in the roots. Who is to say that you can't go after the low-hanging fruit of conversion while simultaneously building a better and longer-lasting foundation, which will bear more branches and higher volumes of fruit? Who is stopping you from planting a second, third, or even fourth tree? What is keeping you from selectively improving the DNA of the tree so that it bears more delicious and low-hanging fruit? And what's the best way to reach the not-so-low-hanging fruit?

These are the kinds of questions most people don't typically ask. But they are the questions that are important to ask when looking to improve conversion. *Convert Every Click* is about questioning your assumptions and looking at your marketing in a different way. It's training yourself to ask the questions and reach for new heights. It's training yourself to see the bigger picture while remembering the individual prospect or customer at the same time.

Ever since I can remember I've been an inherently curious person, which made me a natural experimenter. I loved to take things apart and rebuild them. I also enjoyed building things from scratch. I had many interests and experimented with many projects throughout my life. I've come to realize that most of them contributed to making me into the person I am today.

My father's lifetime hobby has always been the art of performance magic. When I was eight, he brought me into his hobby and exposed me to a world of concepts that most people don't learn in a lifetime. Having to go on stage and present an illusion at age eight was a nerve-wracking experience. Any performance is an art with many parts. As a presenter, you focus not just on yourself, but also on what your audience perceives. Your perception and your audience's perception are totally different things. Every individual has different needs and wants, and so it's the performer's job to try to give each of them what they are looking for. These lessons I learned so young became very valuable later in life with conversion rate optimization.

Around the same time I was learning magic, I was exposed to our first home computer. Because of my keen sense of curiosity, my first thoughts with the computer were *How does this work?* and *What are all the things it can do?* I quickly learned almost everything it could do, and even took it apart and put it back together. My parents didn't love finding that out. Luckily, it still functioned afterward, and apparently I learned some useful skills. A few years later, when I was 11, I made my first business website. At 13, I took on my first e-commerce client.

From ages 13 to 24, I created many different businesses. I spent time as a web programmer and as a print and web designer, and I was always learning how to be a better entrepreneur through each of my businesses.

I also studied psychology and learned more about its profound effect on business and marketing. Because of my need to experiment and figure things out, I went from business to business, learning many skills and gaining exposure to many industries along the way. Because of my early exposure to technology, I always had a special knack for understanding the intricacies of the online world. One of my old employers called me a "triple threat" because of my skills in web design, coding, *and* marketing. Most importantly, because of my entrepreneurial experiences and studies in psychology, I came to understand and greatly appreciate how each of these skills plays a role in generating a good return on investment from every effort, both online and off-line.

Since then, I've built a series of "Core" companies, which fill different needs for different audiences. ConversionCore is a consulting firm that focuses on using my holistic conversion techniques to help mid- to large-sized companies grow their bottom lines. My other companies include ClickCore (an ROI-focused web development company), AutomationCore, which helps small businesses grow through marketing automation–related products, and a few sideline software companies, which solve different problems for different audiences. One of those software companies was acquired, and in 2012 became my first seven-figure deal.

It all comes back to psychology and experimentation. I could never have sold that software company or helped grow so many of my clients' companies without all of the lessons and skills I learned through the years. None of that would have been possible without my natural curiosity and need to continually improve existing systems.

Fortunately for everyone, technology has advanced to the point where you can often use software to test your ideas in the real world and see if you're improving. You don't have to deconstruct and reconstruct entire businesses to achieve improvements. I'll tell you about the software later in the book.

The business world is slowly catching on to these conversion techniques, and I hope they will become mainstream someday. For now, I want to give you a serious competitive edge over other companies. In this book, I'm not just going to tell you how to perform the magic, as if it were a memorized trick. I'm going to show you the principles *behind* the magic of conversion rate optimization, the psychology that makes it really work for all kinds of audiences. And just like magic (pun intended), you're going to be amazed at what you can do once you understand the foundations.

Don't get me wrong; magic is only an analogy here. We're not trying to *trick* people into buying your products or signing up for your mailing list! The goal is to put your products and services in the best light, present them at the best angle, so each audience member sees it in the best possible way for them.

This whole book is about revealing those secrets to you. Starting in the next chapter, I hope your eyes will be opened to a whole new perspective of the online world. Even if you think you already have a pretty good handle on your business, you're going to see something new. But before we can begin, it's important for you and I to be on the same page about what conversion rate optimization is from my perspective.

Let's Start at the Beginning

Even if you already know a good deal about conversion rate optimization (CRO), you're going to find that I approach things a little differently. At some point, CRO became known for on-page optimization, and the industry grew around that. People even now work in isolation, one page at a time. Once they get results for that single page, they move on to the next page.

The problem is that no single marketing component works in isolation. Everything affects something else. It's an entire ecosystem of marketing. When you tinker with one piece by itself, you may have no idea what you're affecting down the line. A boost in conversion rates on one page might actually hurt the bottom line, if you're not paying attention to the bigger picture.

Holistic Conversion Rate Optimization (HCRO), on the other hand, takes the entire marketing ecosystem into account. We like to think in terms of the entire marketing process, including funnels and overall structures. While we do look at individual pages and metrics, we always look at them while simultaneously considering the big picture. In other words, in addition to optimizing the website, we look at what happens before prospects hit the website (traffic), as well as what happens after they leave (follow-up). I call this the Holistic Conversion Timeline

Holistic Conversion Timeline

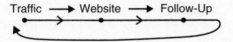

Traffic ⟶ Website ⟶ Follow-Up

Figure 1.1   I look at the conversion process as a timeline. Improving conversions on a web page is good, but improving conversions all along the timeline (including the traffic and follow-up phases) is better.

(Figure 1.1). The traffic stage happens at the beginning of the timeline on the left, then people progress to the website, then there's a follow-up stage. The follow-up takes them back to the traffic stage. There may be other steps in between these three major points on the timeline, such as phone calls or direct mail.

A conversion can happen anywhere on the timeline. For example, if you have an online ad with a phone number, a person might convert into a customer without ever getting to the website. Or if you collect a lead on the website and you have off-line follow-up, they might convert on the follow-up end of things.

In my opinion, the goal should be to lift your overall revenue and/ or profit, even if that means doing something counterintuitive, such as *lowering* a certain conversion point. This big-picture, or timeline, view of CRO is one of the main reasons why I've been fortunate enough to have over 90 percent increases in conversion rates for my clients. It's also the reason why I was strongly encouraged to write this book.

Another component of HCRO is the concept of trying to convert *all* visitors. Traditional CRO typically seeks to optimize for the largest group of people only. But that still leaves out people who might convert, if they were presented with a different experience or offering. So, HCRO solves this problem by optimizing the entire business from a customer-centric perspective. We essentially create a unique optimized experience for every visitor, or as close to it as we can get. The more we lean toward a truly customer-centric and dynamic website, the closer we get to converting all people who come in contact with your business.

You're going to be amazed at all the ways you can grow your business using HCRO. But we need to go over a few terms and concepts before we can dive into all the other cool stuff I want to show you.

What Is Conversion, Anyway?

A conversion is nothing more than a transition from one state of being to another. You can convert from one religion to another. You can convert from one career to another. You can convert a cold call into a hot lead. You can convert a lead into a sale. It's a change from one thing to another.

Although the most obvious examples of conversion may revolve around religion or politics, it's no different in the world of business and online conversion. The goal is to transition anonymous people (your web traffic) into something more useful to you (leads, customers, or raving fans).

A conversion online can be pretty much anything you want it to be. It's the tipping point where a goal is reached. That can be a link clicked, a page read, a form submitted, a purchase made—anything that moves a person closer to your ultimate goal. Because this is a business book, let's assume that ultimate goal is probably to make more money (or to collect donations or spread education in the case of nonprofits).

Good. Now we know what a conversion is. But what is a conversion rate, and why should you optimize it? A basic conversion rate definition is the ratio of conversions over traffic. In other words, how many people saw a certain product divided by how many people bought it (if a purchase was the goal).

So if 100 people saw your web page for lawn furniture and 30 people purchased a set, then the conversion rate is 30 of 100—30/100, or 30 percent. This is just a basic example. There are many ways to define a conversion rate. We'll go over that in more detail later.

Some people believe the term *conversion rate optimization* was influenced by the widely popular term *search engine optimization* (SEO). People who practice SEO are optimizing their web pages so that they rank higher on search engines such as Google. The goal is to get the page as high as possible in the natural or organic (free) search results. People found over time you could do certain things to improve your page's odds of showing up first, or at least higher up in the results.

SEO has become a cutthroat business in some circles. Those who figure out a system that works can make millions of dollars from their kitchen table. Optimizing is their job. They research keywords, tweak copy, and manipulate their web pages all in the quest for traffic. CRO is just another kind of optimizing, but instead of optimizing for the search engines, you optimize for conversions—more sales, more leads, more clicks, whatever you define as a conversion goal. Where SEO is about getting more traffic, CRO is about making more money.

This idea is nothing new. Technically, conversion rates have been around for a long time. Think back 50 years to the days when door-to-door salesmen were common. If they were good, they probably carefully monitored how many people they talked to (their traffic) and how many of those people bought an encyclopedia set or vacuum cleaner (their conversion). If they were good, the ratio of how many people bought versus how many people they spoke to could be considered a conversion rate.

If they spoke to 100 people, and 10 people bought, they'd have a 10 percent conversion rate. That might be pretty respectable, or it might be horrible. It all depends on what they're selling and who their target market is. If their conversions were particularly low, they might study someone more successful to learn better ways of selling, or they might tweak their sales pitch to relate better to the individuals they're talking to. In other words, they'd be creating a more customer-centric experience in order to make more sales.

Most successful businesspeople are continually optimizing for better conversions, whether they know it or not. It's how they improve and grow. Conversion rate optimization brings the same idea of improving conversions into the modern world of the online marketplace. But unlike the old days when everything relied on trial and error, we now have the technology to run tests and know for sure whether one sales pitch is working better than another. The direct-mail world runs tests all the time, but it can take weeks or months to show results. With online CRO, sometimes we can have the answer in just a matter of minutes.

The basic process works like this:

Step 1: Make a change to a web page or a step in your sales funnel.
Step 2: Test the new version against the old version, using special software.
Step 3: Wait to see which version returns more conversions. (The software tracks this automatically.)
Step 4: Keep the winner, and start over from the beginning with a new idea or change.

It's important to keep track of everything you're doing because one small tweak can affect other things way down the line in the sales process. With a good CRO understanding, or a smart consultant on your side, you can put systems in place to tweak and test all aspects of your marketing. It may not happen overnight, but I've seen even small changes to text or pictures on a web page bring about huge lifts in conversion. Even if you start testing without knowing what you're doing, just the act of testing things will help you start to see results.

Conversion Rate Optimization Is Not the Same as Usability

I want to make a quick distinction between conversion rate optimization and usability. It's important to mention here because they can seem similar. They do have overlap, but I believe it's a dangerous notion to think they are the same. I've seen people get tripped up by this and miss out on major opportunities. I've also seen people make usability changes in the name of profit and growth, and they wound up hurting conversions and negatively affecting their bottom line. However, I also know from experience that usability can also improve conversions.

The goal for usability is to make things easier for the user or visitor. The goal for CRO is to get more conversions and thus more money. They can sound the same, but they're not quite. When you make things easier for the user, you can sometimes hurt your bottom line. For example, we've tested strategies where we intentionally made things harder for the user and conversion rates went way up. You may be wondering how this could happen. In theory, conversion rates should go up if you make it easier for the visitor to buy, but that's not always the case.

About 80 percent of CRO overlaps with usability. But that 10 percent on either side of the overlap makes a huge difference (Figure 1.2). When people approach CRO like usability, they spend all their time focused on smoothing out the obstacles in the visitor experience. They try to make it as easy as possible for the visitor to buy. Although that might lead to higher conversions, it may not lead to the most *profitable* conversions.

This practice of smoothing the path, so to speak, is really in the realm of usability. For a company such as Zappos, where the goal is to keep the customer happy at almost any cost, usability may be smart. Keeping customers happy positively affects their bottom line because it is the core

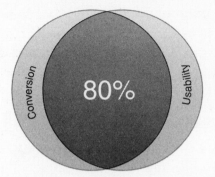

Figure 1.2 **Conversion and usability do have a lot of overlap, but paying attention to the 10 percent on either side can make a huge difference to your bottom line.**

of their business model and has led to great exposure. For example, they offer free shipping even though someone back in 2000 would have said it's totally inefficient and hurts the bottom line. In hindsight, we know that investment paid off.

Sometimes, to bring about a better conversion rate, you need to guide the visitor where *you* want them to go. Think about the shopping experience in an IKEA store. IKEA controls the complete customer journey, right down to arrows on the floor telling you where to go. There's a certain walkway you pretty much have to follow, and that walkway leads you past all of IKEA's displays (Figure 1.3). The floor plan forces every individual customer to see just about everything that is for sale. You can't easily skip over anything. This is a very conversion-focused idea.

Both Zappos and IKEA have dramatically different approaches, but both are highly successful.

Now think about shopping in someplace like Walmart. There you're allowed to go wherever you want, and they try to make it as easy as possible with store features such as wide aisles and plenty of checkout stands. Plenty of people go through Walmart without walking past every single thing they have for sale (Figure 1.4).

IKEA is known for their great customer experience. People love shopping there; because of the way the store is laid out, customers tend to buy more. Most don't realize they're being led through a carefully planned experience. If they do realize it, they don't mind. In most cases,

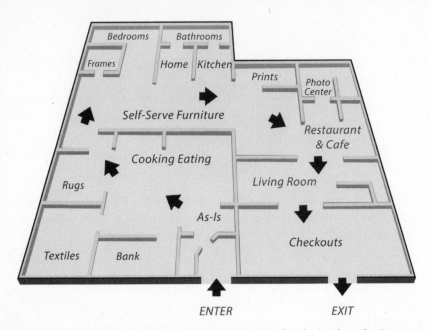

Figure 1.3   IKEA leads its customers through the desired path. Everyone gets the same experience. It's a highly optimized floor plan where the prospect is essentially forced to see everything.

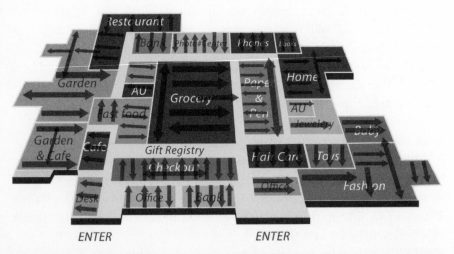

Figure 1.4   Unlike IKEA, stores like Walmart let people wander around the store as they desire. If the visitors do not already know the store layout, it can be confusing to find what they need. Both models work for the individual stores depending on their goals.

they love it and even become raving fans because of it. Thinking traditionally, IKEA is making things more difficult, but so what? Customers enjoy the experience all the same (or even more) and wind up buying more because of it.

If you've ever been involved in sales, you know sometimes customers don't know what they want. Sometimes it takes longer to present what you have to sell, and you have to direct their path so that they see everything they need to see in order to make a purchase decision. Sometimes web sales can improve if you don't make things overly accessible.

Different Types of Conversion Points

If the goal is to convert someone, there has to be a point at which that happens. It's called, conveniently enough, a conversion point. Just about any goal can be considered a conversion point, even something as small as clicking over from an e-mail to a landing page or browsing to the next page of a blog post. But there are some common types of conversion points that you need to be familiar with. There are plenty of other ways conversions can be measured, but these are five of the most common ones.

1. Opt-ins
2. Clicking
3. Purchases
4. Call-ins
5. Engagement

Opt-ins are probably the most popular types of conversion points because they're easy to measure and they represent an important step in many sales processes. An opt-in happens when there's an exchange of information—you offer something in exchange for the visitor's contact information. Typically, at a minimum, you want to collect the person's e-mail address. Most people think of an opt-in as someone opting in to request information from you. The way I like to think of it is people are identifying themselves to you in exchange for your offer. They are raising a hand and identifying themselves as prospects to be engaged and sold. Your job is to find more ways to get people to raise their hands. In fact,

Figure 1.5 An opt-in refers to the act of someone opting in to receive something from you, to be added to your list, or to buy something from you. The opt-in is typically collected through a web form, such as the basic one shown here.

that's the conversion they are making. They convert from an anonymous visitor to a prospect (or lead), a real person who has entered a sales process.

You have a job to do with providing the right incentive for the opt-in. People are most likely not going to do it on their own just because they like you. The opt-in isn't just about them giving you their information. It's about giving them something worthwhile to get them to reciprocate. You have to persuade them to give you the info.

Opt-ins are usually made through a web form of some sort (Figure 1.5). The form may have only one field, such as e-mail address, or it may have many fields. I've seen forms more than 85 questions long! There are distinct strategies for building web forms and optimizing for maximum conversion. We'll start exploring that topic in Chapter 3.

Clicking is how we get around on the web. We click from one page to another or to get from an e-mail to an article. We're constantly clicking links to take us where we want to go (Figure 1.6a). In this case, the conversion is the physical click. This conversion point will sometimes be referred to as a *click-through rate* (CTR) in pay-per-click advertising or an *open rate* for opening and clicking into e-mail. But no matter what you

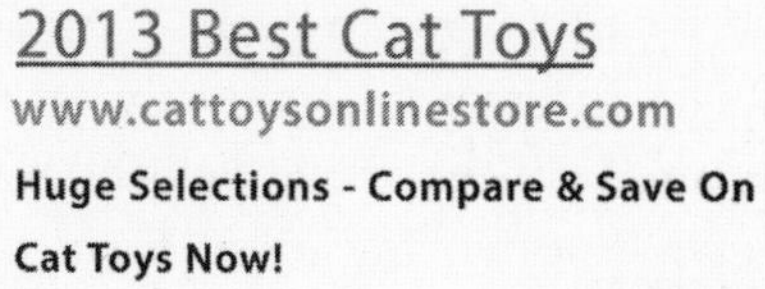

2013 Best Cat Toys
www.cattoysonlinestore.com

Huge Selections - Compare & Save On

Cat Toys Now!

Figure 1.6a This is an example of a paid advertisement that might come up on Google when you search for "cat toys." A click can be considered a conversion point. In this case it is known as a click-through rate (CTR).

Figure 1.6b Typically purchases are made with a button such as the one show here.

call it, every click is a small conversion. Clicks provide valuable information and can move people along the conversion path, if skillfully applied. If not skillfully applied, a click can kill your conversion completely, such as when you include unnecessary outbound links on a sales page, and people click away instead of buying.

A *purchase* is an obvious conversion point, considering that making money is probably the ultimate goal here. There are lots of ways to make a purchase: order forms, shopping carts, mail-in, phone-in, in-person, and in-store. In most cases, a conversion is achieved when someone buys at least one thing. After that, the person may buy something else, but that person has still technically converted.

A *phone call* can also be a conversion point. Some business models rely heavily on a phone bank of sales reps to close the deal. I've had a good number of clients who use hundreds of sales reps. In this case, their main metric for conversion is the *call-in*. For them, success is based on the number of people who call in after visiting their website, how many convert into customers via the phone, and how much each step in the process costs them.

Engagement can also be a conversion point. Engagement is the act of getting a website visitor to interact in some way on the site. This could be navigating anywhere else on the same website, watching a video, or depending on the business model, any other form of interaction that's important to the business owner. This is typical with businesses that sell advertising on their websites, such as blogs and gaming sites.

Smaller Steps May Be Necessary

For every conversion point you may have, there can be many smaller steps leading up to it. We call these microconversion points.

What Do People Do When They Find Your Website?

- Do they browse around for a while?
- Do they buy something?
- Do they sign up for your newsletter or a free report?
- Do they just click the back button on their browser without even reading your site?

They probably do a combination of these. (And if you just don't know about any of this, then I'm really glad you're reading this book!)

More important, what do you *want* them to do? What's the goal? Every page on your website should have a goal, even if that goal is just to have visitors click through to the next page or the next article. Each goal is a microstep on the way to your larger, ultimate goal of making a sale or collecting a lead. Each microstep can also be a conversion point. Visitors may go from your home page to your product page. If people sign up for your newsletter, they convert from being anonymous visitors to known leads. You now know something useful about them, such as their first name and e-mail address. These small steps are called microconversions, and they are very important, especially if you're selling something expensive or relatively unknown to your target audience.

If you're selling sailboats, it's very important to educate visitors over time. People don't generally whip out their credit card to buy a sailboat the first time they see a website. It's a decision that takes education and trust built over time. It's usually a longer sales cycle. So it's probably in your best interest to make sure you have at least their e-mail address before they leave your site. With that one piece of information in your hand, you can continue the conversation about your awesome boats through e-mail or other strategies, such as direct mail. It all depends on what other contact information you have on them. In this case, that microconversion is very important. It's important enough to measure carefully.

Bottom Line Conversion Is What Counts

If we're talking about microconversions as steps in a process leading to an ultimate goal, that ultimate goal is an increase in the bottom line. It's how much money goes into your pocket at the end of the day. That's the whole reason you want to optimize, right? When talking about the bottom line in CRO, we're talking about the revenue from the ultimate conversion point, or ideally even the net profit. I call this number the Bottom Line Conversion Rate.

Let's take a look at the imaginary sailboat website again. If 100 people come to the web page and only one person buys, there's a 1 percent conversion rate. That rate might be okay, but the company owners would like to do better. So, they make some changes here and there. Maybe they changed the pictures on the page, or made the order button bigger, or improved the descriptions a bit. If two people buy, the company now has a 2 percent conversion rate. In theory, they just doubled their income without paying any more for advertising or traffic generation. Sweet!

You may have heard other CRO consultants explain microconversions from a mathematical perspective. In theory, from a mathematical standpoint, each microconversion lift adds to the next point in the process. So, if you increase the conversions in one step by 10 percent, you are theoretically increasing the bottom line by 10 percent.

Unfortunately, it doesn't work that way. In reality, not every microconversion lift is going to improve your bottom line. It's taught this way because it's an assumption that is often made in order to serve as a clear measurement of the optimization and testing process. However, the actual results vary.

For example, if you get more people to click from Google to a landing page, that's good, right? You should get an income boost. But if that landing page isn't converting well, then your bottom line may not go up. In fact, if you get the wrong people clicking through because your targeting is off, you could wind up paying for useless traffic and your bottom line could go down.

The reality of CRO is there are almost always variables at play that make it not perfectly quantifiable. They don't always fit nicely in a math equation. We're measuring human behavior, and behavior isn't an exact science. Microconversions are still important and do contribute to the bottom line. It's important to remember that microconversions can have a domino effect (good or bad) on other conversions later in your sales process.

That's one of the reasons my consulting firm does things differently than other CRO companies out there. That's why we often use the term *Holistic Conversion Rate Optimization*.

What Is Holistic CRO?

It's important to look at the big picture, including the traffic stage (what happens before visitors get to the website) and the follow-up stage (what happens after they leave the website). Sometimes better online sales mean lower off-line or e-mail sales. How can that happen? Very easily. Imagine you sell beds online. You sell the most beautiful, most comfortable, most amazing beds ever. You make a good living, but you hear about this "new" CRO thing and decide to give it a try. So you make changes to your website that lift conversion of first-time website visitors to an all-time high of 36 percent. You're thrilled! You're making more money online than you ever have before. You start planning that cruise to the Bahamas you promised your family when you first opened the business.

But hold on a minute. Part of your sales process (your funnel) included direct mail. Before you made the change, people would come to your site and want a bit more education before deciding to purchase. They would call you up and ask questions. Then they'd think about it for a while. In the meantime, you sent them some direct-mail postcards, which had a high conversion rate. People would get the postcard in the mail and go back to your website. But now they find a website that doesn't match the look or the offering on the postcard. They get confused and don't buy.

You wind up *losing* a significant amount of the sales you used to get from the postcards. Your bottom line goes down. Also, it costs a lot of money to print and mail thousands of postcards, so three months later you're trying to figure out why your sales are up but profits are down. Bummer.

Now, this is a hypothetical situation, but in this example the business suffered because they didn't look at *both* the online and off-line components. Another problem with focusing on the microconversions is people tend to get hyperfocused on optimizing one page to death. They tweak and tweak and make tiny changes all over the place, when they might get much higher lifts by going back to the drawing board, being creative, and trying a completely different approach. If you pay attention only to microconversion rates alone with CRO, you could be missing the boat.

I've been involved in scenarios where we quadrupled the size of multimillion-dollar companies in a few months just by looking at things from a holistic perspective. Although that much of a jump is not typical, higher growth paths are much more feasible with Holistic CRO. I believe strongly that HCRO is what has allowed my company to see these kinds of opportunities so often.

Likewise, if you pay attention only to the bottom line conversion rate, you're missing out on a lot of other opportunities because you have no idea what is driving that conversion. If you know what's driving conversion, you can drive it up in other places, too.

HCRO means you look at your entire marketing funnel—your whole platform, online and off-line—before and after people land on a website. They are all part of your process, and they all feed into your bottom line. When we talk conversion with clients, we're paying attention to their *entire* business so we don't miss something important that could lead to huge boosts in income or devastating losses.

It may seem overwhelming to factor in all the variables from dozens, or hundreds, of microconversion variables from all your different marketing streams and wind up with a cohesive plan. But that's exactly what you can do with HCRO. Over time, you'll start to make sense out of the confusion so that the lifts and drops in conversion are measured and understood in terms of the big picture.

Holistic Conversion Pyramid

The key to getting started is in understanding the Holistic Conversion Pyramid (Figure 1.7). This is a model I developed to explain the difference between Holistic CRO methods and traditional CRO methods.

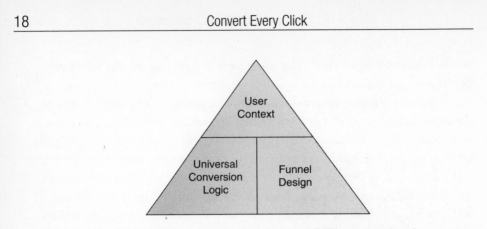

Figure 1.7 The Holistic Conversion Pyramid illustrates the three components to a holistic conversion strategy: Universal Conversion Logic, User Context, and Funnel Design.

There are three components to any holistic strategy:

1. User Context
2. Universal Conversion Logic
3. Funnel Design

What Is Universal Conversion Logic?

Most conversion consultants (and business owners figuring it out for themselves) limit themselves to using what they've read are best practices at first. These are the tips and tools you can find online or in books that tell you things like when to use one color over another color, how many columns to have, or how much white space should be on a page. They're all the techniques people think generally work to lift conversions.

The place I want you to start is called Universal Conversion Logic (UCL). This is the psychology *behind* what makes a red button work on some websites and a green button work on other websites. UCL is why on English-language websites, you may want things to flow left to right, but on Hebrew or Arabic sites, you may consider flowing right to left, for example. Logic suggests people will tend to consume information in the direction they are used to reading. The problem with taking best practices at face value is every site is unique. What worked great for one company might fail miserably for yours. If you don't understand the logic behind the best practice, you won't know why it failed (and you won't know how to fix it).

When working with CRO, most people just stop at the best practices. They don't take into account user context or funnel design. But I'm betting you're smarter than that, so let's look at these other two pieces of the conversion puzzle.

What Is User Context?

User context combines everything about the people behind the screen: who they are, where they came from, where they're sitting, what they know, and what they don't know. It also includes the *setting* of the audience and their *intention* or reason for being on your website.

- Are they sitting in front of a desktop computer at work or browsing on their iPad?
- Are they searching to buy a product to solve a particular problem, or are they just surfing around looking for information?
- Have they been to a website like this before and have certain expectations?
- Are they experienced with websites like yours or are they novices?
- Where are they coming from: a search engine or a media campaign?
- How close are they to being ready to buy?

These details are all part of user context. The more you know about the context of the user, the more customer-centric you're able to get.

Every person is different. Take my wife, Jenna, and me, for instance. We are individuals, with different strengths and weaknesses, different learning styles and buying behaviors. We both process information and make decisions differently. If you put us each in front of a computer and give us a task, we're both going to solve the problem in different ways. (And, really, I might just delegate the task to someone else entirely.)

The user context plays a big part in what conversion logic you may want to use to lift conversions.

What Is Funnel Design?

Your funnel is essentially your marketing and sales process. It's a series of steps that lead the visitor through your website or other marketing and sales tactics toward the ultimate conversion point or goal. You might have several funnels, depending on your business model. Funnels include your microconversions and a bottom line conversion rate (Figure 1.8).

Sales and Marketing Funnel/Process

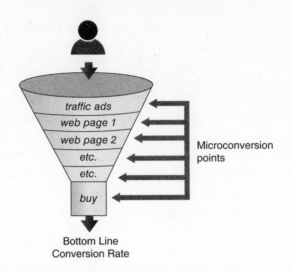

Figure 1.8 **A funnel is your sales and marketing process. In order to have a good understanding of your funnel(s), it's important to know all the steps a person takes from your traffic source, through your website, and all the way down to the Bottom Line Conversion Point.**

I've found that user context and funnel design are the most important things to understand and are the least understood, even in the CRO industry. These concepts create a framework from which to run tests and improve your bottom line. When you intentionally consider all three parts of the pyramid equally, you are starting to think more holistically about CRO.

As we dive deeper into various conversion strategies and techniques, remember to keep all three elements of the pyramid in mind. Designing your funnel is the first step (we'll be getting to that in the next chapter). You're going to need to know as much of your user's context as possible to do a good job. After that, you will want to consider user context again for each microconversion point you decide to optimize. Finally, you will use your knowledge of Universal Conversion Logic to help more users move through your funnel.

Now that you know what HCRO is, the next chapter will dive deeper into the first piece of the Holistic Conversion Pyramid: creating effective funnels.

Build Your Skills

The skills lab for this chapter will help you practice coming up with the user context for your own company.

You can find this skills lab at www.ConvertEveryClick.com/chapter1

CHAPTER TWO

Designing Your Funnel

One of the most common questions I hear from people interested in conversion is "Where do I start?" Theoretically, I could tell them to just make random changes and test the results, and that would be better than nothing. But they need to know where to find the *ideas* for those changes. Where do you look? How do you decide what should change?

In the Holistic CRO model, I tell people to start with the funnel. Get a clear understanding of the big picture—the company's entire marketing process, as well as some of the individual smaller pieces. What does it look like for someone to come into the process and then turn into a customer? What does that experience look like? Larger companies and legacy websites often have more complicated funnels and systems that are difficult to see clearly. This does not make the value of understanding the funnel any less valid, just more challenging. I've often challenged people in those situations to perhaps consider simplifying the funnel. In my experience, doing so has almost always led to better results. Once they can see the funnel clearly, it's easier to find the areas that can be improved.

As we learned in the last chapter, funnel design is one of the three pieces of the Holistic Conversion Pyramid, and it's usually where I start with clients. It's important to understand what your funnel looks like in order to decide on any changes that might lead to higher conversion rates.

What Is a Funnel?

A funnel is a theoretical marketing and sales model that describes the process or journey that a prospect takes to becoming a customer. Marketing people describe it as a funnel because the overall shape looks kind of like a kitchen funnel. You want to gather a lot of people from a wide variety of sources and send them into the wide top of the funnel. Then, steps in the sales process move them progressively toward the bottom of the funnel. Unlike a real funnel, though, not everyone makes it to the bottom. People (most often the majority of people) disappear in the middle.

The goal is to get as many people as possible from the top to the bottom. The journey can be a fast-moving freeway, funneling lots of people through easily and efficiently to their destination. Or it can be a twisting, winding, barely visible series of trails in a dense forest—full of wrong turns, dead ends, and interesting distractions. The overall effect is that lots of people enter, and only some make it out the other side.

Unfortunately, many funnels look like Swiss cheese, with gaping holes that leak traffic. In other words, they're leaking money. The good news is that this is where huge opportunities often exist.

Let's take a look at the most common shapes of funnels:

- *Standard Funnel:* The standard funnel shape (Figure 2.1) is what people tend to *think* their funnels look like. It's the shape they are familiar with—wide at the top, narrow at the bottom. More traffic comes in, and less traffic converts and comes out the bottom. It's pretty simple to understand.

Standard
Funnel

Figure 2.1 If a businessperson is thinking about funnels at all, that's a good thing. Most of them think they have a standard funnel setup, but that's not usually the case.

- *Typical Funnel:* The typical funnel (Figure 2.2) is what most businesses *actually* have in place. This is where things start to go wrong. Companies take all sorts of marketing tools and just stick them together. They might think they have a funnel, but they don't. Instead of a logical progression of steps leading the visitor toward the goal, they have a tangled-up maze. Some people manage to make it out of the maze and convert but not nearly as many as there could be.
- *Concave Funnel:* This is another common problem funnel. I also call this one the traffic or AdWords funnel because it's what sometimes happens with companies driving traffic using pay-per-click (PPC) agencies. This funnel might start out okay, looking more or less like a standard funnel, but these agencies or "traffic experts" focus on pouring more and more traffic in, which makes the funnel top heavy (Figure 2.3). Basically, they widen out the top so much that it develops concave sides. This distortion makes the funnel much less efficient.

You might look at your website and say, "We have a 40 percent conversion rate. How do we make more money?" The common answer is to drive more traffic. In theory that makes sense. But the wider the top gets, the less efficiently the funnel works. A 200 percent increase in traffic might only give you a 50 percent gain in your bottom line conversion rate. Now, don't get me wrong; you can still make millions of dollars doing that. It's how a lot of the big companies make so much money. They have huge ad budgets and tiny conversion rates.

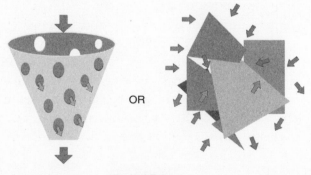

OR

Typical Funnel

Figure 2.2 A typical funnel is not clear, no matter how you look at it. It is either full of holes, like Swiss cheese, and leaks traffic and money, or it is so confusing, it might as well be Swiss cheese. There are many paths for visitors to enter and exit the funnel, and the process is not well designed.

Concave (Traffic) Funnel

Figure 2.3 A concave funnel illustrates what happens when you add traffic with the assumption that you will add conversions at the same rate. That's not what happens in reality.

But if they focused a little more on conversion rate optimization *inside* the funnel, a higher percentage of the traffic they poured in would wind up converting. Reshaping or fixing a concave funnel can make a huge difference to your profits, especially if you have a large advertising budget.

Whether you've never thought about designing a funnel for your business at all or you now realize you have some problems with your funnel, it's okay. We're going to learn how to fix that in this book. What you want to aim for is what I call a Lean Funnel.

Aim for a Lean Funnel

When you have an optimized funnel that operates smoothly and has a good conversion rate, you've created a lean funnel (Figure 2.4).

Basically, you're using conversion rate optimization techniques to widen out the bottom of a standard funnel. When you do this, more of your traffic makes it to the bottom and your conversion rates increase. You might do this by adding a step or two in your sales process, removing some unnecessary steps, or just tidying things up. You're creating a smoother progression through the funnel, and in the process, optimizing for more conversions. This is the ideal funnel shape; it's what you want to shoot for.

Building a Lean Funnel from Scratch

Start by thinking about the big picture. How do people get from point A (total strangers) to point B (identified leads) to point C (customers)?

Lean Funnel

Figure 2.4   A Lean Funnel has better proportions. The higher the percentage of people you convert in your funnel, the wider the bottom becomes in proportion to the top opening.

An easy way to start is by identifying the top and the bottom steps first and then filling in the middle steps:

- The top step is the traffic source. How will people enter the funnel?
- The bottom step is the goal. What do you want them to do?
- The middle steps are all the things that need to happen to get to the goal. There may be only one or two middle steps, or there may be many. It all depends on your business. However, try to keep the progression logical and simple. Don't add extra steps you don't need unless it's strategic.

Two of the most common funnels are ones that convert a person from visitor to lead (a lead funnel) and lead to customer (a sales funnel). You may need one or the other, or you may need both. It all depends on your business.

Here's an example. Let's say you sell high-end, expensive kitchenware. Here's what the lead and sales funnels might look like.

Lead funnel: Converting visitor to lead
Traffic source: PPC advertising
Goal: Sign up for free report

Steps to the goal:
1. Search online for "kitchenware."
2. Click on PPC ad and go to landing page.
3. Fill out a web form for free report.

Sales funnel: Converting lead to customer
Traffic: List of people who signed up for free report
Goal: Make a sale
Steps to the goal:
1. Receive report and read it.
2. Open e-mails about the product or relevant topics.
3. Click to view a certain product. (This click might come from a link inside the online report itself or a follow-up e-mail sent later.)
4. View product page.
5. Click Add to Cart.
6. Click Checkout.
7. Fill in billing and shipping details.
8. Click to submit order.

Some of the preceding steps in the sales funnel might get skipped, but the funnel is still valid. For example, visitors may skip step two and just buy.

Two Strategies to Easily Optimize Common Funnel Flaws

If you're already in business and making sales online, you probably have a typical (jumbled-up) funnel or an AdWords funnel. You're going to want to fix your funnel and make it resemble the lean funnel as closely as possible. There are lots of ways to fix a funnel. Following are two techniques I use to fix my clients' funnels.

Solving the Plinko® Problem with Linear Funnels Let me explain this strategy using the game Plinko® to illustrate. If you don't know this game, imagine a vertical board full of randomly placed pins. At the bottom of the board is a small bucket labeled *Got 'em!* You're going to drop a plastic chip from somewhere on the top of the board and try to get it to land in that bucket.

If you're lucky—you guess the right starting point, the chip doesn't get stuck, and it drops the way you hope it will—you might just hit the jackpot. *Lucky. Guess. Hope. Might.* These words don't offer very good odds, but you're optimistic. Besides, if the first chip doesn't make it, you can always buy more and try again.

You drop one chip after another into one of the entry points to the board. Each one bounces back and forth through the pins, snaking its way down toward the bucket. You win some; you lose some (see Figure 2.5).

That's all well and good if you're playing the carnival game, but when you're spending money to acquire customers and sending them through your marketing maze, ideally you want them *all* to land in the Got 'em bucket and become customers.

You may not realize it, but this is what's happening every time a person enters your funnel. You hope you get lucky and the prospect bounces through the pins in the right order and eventually winds up becoming a customer. But the reality is, most times the person ends up in the Lost 'em bucket or simply falls on the floor.

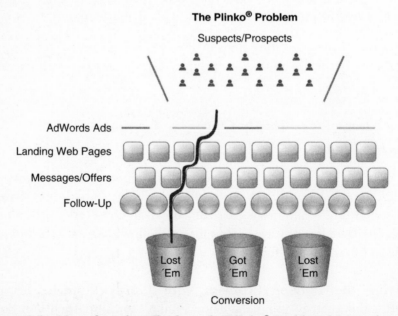

Figure 2.5   Many funnels suffer from the Plinko® Problem. Visitors bounce around the pages of a website or other advertising, and only a small percentage make it to the Got 'em bucket. It's not a very efficient way to run a business.

Plinko® is a registered trademark of Freemantle Media Operations BV.

Why? Because prospects are bounced around the funnel by dozens or even hundreds of disorganized pins—unnecessary clicks, wrong turns, and dead ends. Sometimes visitors make it all the way through and decide not to buy. Much of the time, they simply give up and disappear off the board before they even make it to the bottom.

What if you could rig the game in your favor? What if you could line up the pins so that it was a straight drop from the entry point to the Got 'em bucket? And hey, let's throw a few more Got 'em buckets down at the base to catch even more (Figure 2.6).

This is what I call building Linear Funnels. It's a strategy where you make adjustments to your funnel, just like lining up the pins on the Plinko® board. When the pins line up, it's a linear path straight to the bottom. You drop the chip in at the top, and it slides effortlessly down to the Got 'em bucket.

There are lots of ways to do this. You could fix a concave/traffic funnel with linear funnels by segmenting keywords or ad groups. If you use search engine optimization (SEO), each page on your website could be a separate linear funnel. It's all about dividing your traffic into segments and creating specialized funnels (unique experiences) just for them. When you put them all together, it looks like a series of straws inside your funnel. Because this is such a great technique, the funnel actually expands to hold more. It looks something like Figure 2.7.

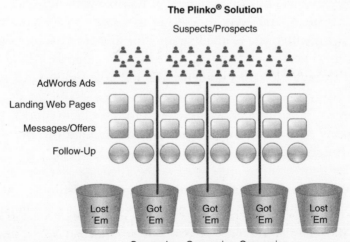

Figure 2.6 The Plinko® Problem can be solved by lining up the pins so people funnel straight down to a conversion (Got 'em!).

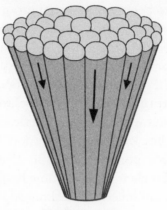

Linear Funnels

Figure 2.7   Linear Funnels look like straws inside a funnel. They are linear paths inside a larger funnel plan, just like straight channels on an optimized Plinko® board.

Now, it can be difficult to line up every pin exactly right for every customer. We are dealing with human behavior, after all. Consumers behave differently depending on their needs, their emotional states, how much money they have to spend, and lots of other factors. But if you know your market and your industry well, and you think with a customer-centric mind-set, you can predict the visitor's behavior and set up marketing that will line up as straight as possible with the goal.

There are several ways to use linear funnels to fix your current funnel. Remember, you're dividing up your funnel into a series of thinner, straight-line funnels. You might use this technique for selling a single product to multiple target audiences or multiple products to multiple audiences.

Creating linear funnels is one way to fix a problem funnel. Another way is using what I call the Double Funnel technique, one of my favorite old-standby tactics. Let's look at that now.

Fix Your Funnel with the Double Funnel Technique   A second way to fix your funnel is to use what I call the Double Funnel technique. It isn't really two funnels; it's more like two parts to one funnel. But because we are talking about using a lead funnel and a sales funnel together in this situation, it's easier to think of them as two. This is often a good place to start when optimizing shopping carts. It almost always leads to major increases in bottom line conversions, and it's relatively easy to implement.

Say you have a product sales page, and you have a traffic stream leading to the page. If people buy, you get them. If they don't buy, they're gone. That's an extremely small, but typical, sales funnel. Are most people going to be ready to buy right away? Probably not, especially if they've never heard of you.

Could you possibly convince them to convert later on through e-mail or direct mail? Maybe. But you'll never get the chance to try if you don't capture some information about them before they leave.

In the Double Funnel technique, we stack the lead funnel on top of the sales funnel. The lead funnel contains a way for visitors to opt in to your mailing list. That means visitors can give you their contact information in return for something relevant you're offering. We almost always add a free, or nearly free, relevant incentive for visitors to give us their information: a free downloadable report, a video series, a tutorial, a coupon—whatever will entice them to sign up. (We'll talk in more detail about exactly what to offer in the next chapter.) Adding this extra funnel can open up possibilities to use follow-up marketing to re-engage visitors not ready to buy. We'll talk more about how to do this in the traffic chapter.

An Example Let's say you make gourmet chocolate and you're selling a Chocolate of the Month Club online. You set up a sales page for it with a nice big Buy Now button. Visitors either buy or they don't. What happens to the people who come to the website and then leave? How many will come back? Experience tells us almost none will return. So, how can you capture their information to keep them in the funnel longer?

There are lots of ways to solve this problem; here's one idea: You could add a step where they sign up to get a free sample mailed to them. (Who doesn't like free chocolate?) People who aren't ready to buy right now aren't risking much by having you send a free sample. All they're doing is giving you their mailing address and maybe an e-mail. That information is gold for conversion purposes. You can now use new strategies like e-mail marketing or direct mail to encourage them to buy later. Maybe you can even convince them to buy subscriptions as gifts for friends and family.

That's one possible solution. But maybe mailing free chocolate is too expensive, and people aren't too keen on giving away their home address. Regardless of the obstacles, there are usually alternative ways to accomplish your goal. In that case, you could simply ask for an e-mail address and send them a *coupon* for free chocolate that they can redeem in a store. That moves them from sitting in front of their computer to standing in front of your chocolate counter picking out what they'd like to buy. Sweet!

This simple double funnel looks like this: Your lead generation funnel starts with advertising that sends people to a web page. On that page, a web form captures their e-mail address in return for a coupon for a free sample. That leads into the sales funnel, which involves them printing out the coupon (or storing it on their mobile phone) and coming into your store, where you sell them lots of delicious treats. There's a smooth transition between the lead funnel and the sales funnel. That's the whole idea of the double funnel.

Building Referrals with an Hourglass Funnel

An audience member once asked me whether funnels always had to start big and end small, or if there were a way to open the funnel back up at the bottom. In reply, I explained the Hourglass Funnel and how it works. An hourglass funnel is used mainly to encourage referrals. It's shaped like an hourglass with a wide top and a wide bottom (Figure 2.8). You send people in at the top, and the ones that convert in the middle bring friends with them at the bottom. It's the process of customers creating more customers.

This funnel should be created deliberately. Accidental referrals can happen, but it's much better if you have a system in place to encourage word of mouth. The funnel might include an e-mail campaign, a Tell a Friend button on your checkout page, a YouTube video, or social media sharing.

A very simple referral funnel for the kitchenware site example I mentioned earlier might look like this:

Traffic: Current customers
Goal: Get new people into the funnel
Steps to the goal:

1. Send e-mail to current customers with a link to a free report. Request that they send the link to friends who like to cook.
2. Send another follow-up e-mail offering their friends a special offer when they request the free report.
3. Repeat this funnel twice a year for special promotions, such as barbecue and holiday gift-giving seasons.

Dropbox.com is a great example of how an hourglass funnel helped create a multimillion-dollar business. Dropbox sells digital storage in the cloud, kind of like using space on the Internet as a place to store large files, videos, photos, and so on. The owners discovered they could build a lot of demand for their product with a well-crafted hourglass funnel. They offer a reward to both sides of the equation, the customer and the referral, with more space to store things in the cloud. According to Dropbox's chief executive officer, Drew Houston, the referral program increased sign-ups 60 percent, and as of 2010 a full 35 percent of sign-ups every day are referrals.

Common Mistakes to Avoid When Building Funnels

- *Don't assume the funnel is bad just because your conversions aren't as high as you'd like.* Implementation is the key here. In most cases, failure happens because the changes you implement in an effort to optimize aren't quite right. Let's say you tried to build a lean funnel where your website visitors travel straight down to your goal. Setting up the funnel is fairly simple. The visitor goes from point A to point B to point C until there's a conversion. It's a simple process on paper. If you fail to get a good conversion rate, it's probably because of some other reason than a bad funnel design. It could be you need more credibility on the page. Maybe your message or call to action isn't quite right. Perhaps you made faulty assumptions about your target audience. There are lots of reasons why conversions are low. This is exactly why there is conversion rate optimization. If you've taken the time to build a funnel on purpose, it's probably fine. Rather than assuming your funnel is at fault, spend some time tweaking your pages and split testing them to find out what's really going on.

Hourglass (Referral) Funnel

Figure 2.8   An Hourglass Funnel is the process of opening the bottom of your funnel by having your customers refer other customers. In essence, it's a customer referral funnel, which behaves as a function of your overall holistic funnel.

- *Don't add in extra steps if they don't serve a strategic purpose.* Streamline your funnels so that they are as efficient as possible. You don't want to leave out important steps in the process, such as educating the prospects on value, but you also don't want them aimlessly clicking around your website when you want them to be filling out the order form.
- *Don't copy a competitor just because you can.* Every business is different. Use competitors as resources for new funnels to test.
- *Don't only look at your industry for funnel designs.* Sometimes the best ideas come from outside your own industry.

Build Your Skills

The skills lab for this chapter will help you practice designing funnels for your own company. You will also find a video tutorial for how to create a lead-generating web form and put it on your website.

You can find this skills lab at www.ConvertEveryClick.com/chapter2

CHAPTER THREE

Information Capture and Defining the Ideal Conversion Point

Information is the currency of the Internet. If you have a website visitor's personal information, the chances of you converting him or her are infinitely greater than your chances of converting an anonymous visitor. Similarly, the more you know about your visitors, the better your chance to "convert every click." So, how do you get the information from them? At what point in the process do you collect it, and what can you do to get them to give you *more* information? And what do you do with the information to move toward converting every click? This chapter is designed to answer those questions. Let's start at the beginning.

What Is Information Capture?

Information capture may sound like cyber-espionage or some cloak-and-dagger scenario, but it's actually one of the most important jobs of your website. Information truly is the currency of the Internet. The more information you have, the more likely you'll be able to turn that information into money at the end of the day.

In a nutshell, information capture is when visitors give you some personal identifying information about themselves, allowing you to keep in contact with them even after they've left your website. Let's define some terms here before we get too deep into this topic. A visitor is any person who comes to any page on your website. There are four types of website visitors: suspects, prospects, leads, and customers. Definitions vary, but for this book, here's what I mean by these terms:

- A *suspect* is an anonymous visitor you have no way of telling if they'll every buy from you.
- A *prospect* is a suspect engaged with you in some way, even if that engagement is only viewing your website. In the context of website visitors, a prospect is an anonymous person who may eventually buy something from you.
- A *lead* is a prospect who has been identified by giving you some information about himself or herself.
- A *customer* is someone who has purchased from you and may do so again.

The key thing to understand here is that suspects and prospects are anonymous, and leads and customers are identified visitors. In other words, you know something personal about them. It might be as simple as their name or e-mail address.

Your goal with information capture is to move as many people as possible across the line from anonymous to identified (Figure 3.1).

Visitors to Your Website

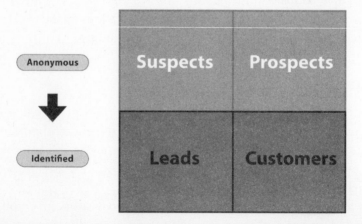

Figure 3.1 Generally, the more people you can identify, the more you can convert into leads and customers. Identification is an important step in the conversion process.

How important is it to identify your visitors? Let's say 1,000 people visit your website and 10 people buy something on their first visit. Out of the other 990 people who didn't buy anything, how many might actually be good leads? How many might need a little more time or a little more information before deciding to buy from you? 100? 300? 800?

Here's the thing—if you don't identify them by capturing at least an e-mail address soon after they land on your website, all those potential leads are gone. If they leave your site, they'll probably never come back, even if they liked what they saw and were searching for a credit card at the exact moment the phone rang and distracted them from buying. (This excludes certain techniques like cookie remarketing, which we'll discuss in the chapter on follow-up marketing.)

You have practically no way of knowing why people leave your site. It could be because they're not interested in what you're offering. But often they simply get distracted, can't find the answer to a question, or don't have time to place an order right then. If you don't take the time to do proper information capture, you're losing all those prospects and leaving money on the table—a *lot* of money.

Remember the Plinko® problem from the last chapter? The people who disappear halfway through or those who just fall on the floor without making it into a bucket might be great leads for you, but you'll never know if you don't get at least an e-mail address from them.

Catching them in a *Got 'em* bucket with information capture means converting them from an anonymous prospect to an identified lead. You want to identify them as fast as possible, preferably *before* they start their way through the rest of your funnel.

Types of Information to Capture

There are many types of information you can capture: name, phone number, gender, company, website—the possibilities are practically endless. But in most online situations, you want to capture visitors' e-mail addresses at a minimum. This gives you the ability to follow up with them later, give them more information about your products, and show them how you can help solve their problems.

In our previous example of those 990 people disappearing off your website and never coming back, imagine if you could get another 30 people to give you their e-mail addresses. Could you get some of them to buy later? Of course you could. But if you don't have that information, all those people are just gone, possibly forever.

Depending on what you're selling, the sales cycle can last from a few seconds to several years. Generally, the more complex or expensive your offering, the longer the sales cycle and the more you need to stay in contact with every prospect. People used to say you couldn't sell expensive, long-cycle products, such as manufacturing machinery, online. But that's just not true. It might take a sophisticated funnel with several working parts, including information capture, a powerful e-mail marketing campaign, and even dedicated sales staff, but it's possible.

If you are selling long-cycle products or services that take months or years to close the deal, it's even more important to identify the leads who are the most likely to buy. Information capture gives you a way to screen out the time wasters from the truly hot leads.

How Do You Capture Information?

The most common way to capture information is to use a web form. These forms can be used to capture a lead or a sale. Most websites capture information on an order form during a sales transaction. Here they find out the visitor's name, address, credit card details, and so on, but it's better if you can capture at least some of that information much earlier. Web forms are easily created with drag-and-drop tools provided by most e-mail marketing platforms, such as Constant Contact, AWeber, Infusionsoft, Eloqua, Exact Target, and Marketo. You can also have a web developer build you a custom form, but you still want to have a database somewhere to hold all the information you're collecting. And you want to do something with the information in the database, not just collect it.

Fully automated marketing systems, such as Infusionsoft (targeted at small businesses), are sophisticated tools with tagging systems that let you identify your visitors based on whatever criteria you want to name. You can tag people as "married dog lovers who live in the city" and market to them with targeted messages that are different from the messages you send to "single cat lovers who live in the country."

If you use a call center, you can direct people to call in and then capture their information over the phone. This can work well, depending on your market, but people need to be motivated to pick up the phone. A web form is a low-level investment in terms of time and personal interaction. A well-designed web form doesn't need to take a lot of time or energy to fill out. As long as you have the right incentive for visitors to fill it out, they probably will.

What Information Do You Need to Capture?

The answer depends on how you plan to follow up. There are many different ways to follow up and convert people—e-mail, phone, direct mail, text message, and so on. Most of the time, you're only going to collect the data you plan to use. It's good to have as much data as possible on people, but there's a danger you could scare them away by asking for too much or too personal information. If you usually communicate with prospects through e-mail, there's probably no reason to ask for their phone number right at the start. If you plan to use phone follow-up, you probably don't need their physical mailing address right away. Starting with a simple e-mail capture is common and effective because people don't usually mind giving away an e-mail address.

You can ask for just about any information you want on your web form, not just contact data. You can ask for demographic data, such as their age, sex, or income level. You can ask for psychographic data, such as their hobbies, interests, and opinions. You can even find out transactional data, such as what their specific problem is, what they're looking for, or when they plan to make a purchase. Some pieces of information you can capture without having to ask at all, such as an estimate of their location based on the computer's IP address.

Gathering the best and most detailed information means you are starting to build a more customer-centric business. You're looking at individual customers and learning as much as you can about them without scaring them away. This is important because it can be easier to persuade and sell to them later on. Ideally, you want to capture as many details as possible, but you have to balance all the details you want with what people are willing to give you. If they feel like you're asking for too much, or it takes too much time to fill out your form, they probably won't bother.

Types of Web Forms for Information Capture

There are many types of web forms you can use to capture information. Which type you choose to use and how you implement it can have a large impact on how many people will fill it out. There is a strategy to choosing your forms. Let's look at the pros and cons of some of the more common varieties, and then I'll show you a couple of my favorite advanced strategies.

Long Capture Web Forms

These were the first web form technique used by online businesses. They are lengthy forms usually available on contact pages or order forms, and typically include six or more fields, which can be any kind—checkboxes, text fields, radio buttons, and so on (Figure 3.2).

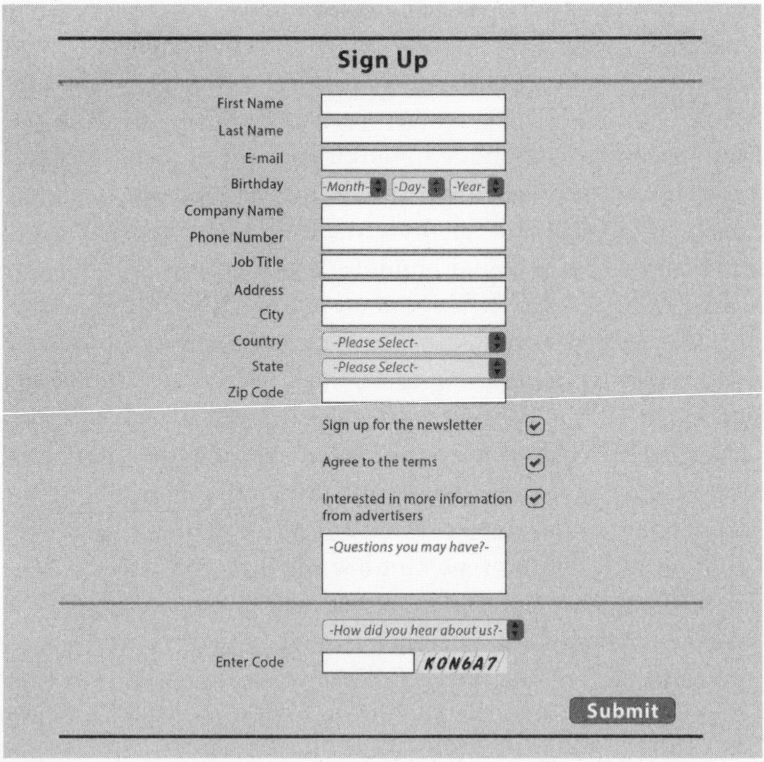

Sign Up

First Name	
Last Name	
E-mail	
Birthday	-Month- -Day- -Year-
Company Name	
Phone Number	
Job Title	
Address	
City	
Country	-Please Select-
State	-Please Select-
Zip Code	

Sign up for the newsletter ☑

Agree to the terms ☑

Interested in more information ☑
from advertisers

-Questions you may have?-

-How did you hear about us?-

Enter Code   KON6A7

Submit

Figure 3.2 Long capture forms can be daunting to fill out, and that can hurt conversion rates. There are techniques for collecting lots of information without sacrificing conversions, including short-to-long capture, multistep, and smooth capture forms, which we will start discussing shortly.

There's a lot to fill out with long capture forms, which can be over-whelming. A good example of one is a single-page order form where you ask for name, e-mail, phone, billing address, shipping address, credit card information, and so on. That alone can be 25 fields or more. It means the visitor has to *really* want to make that purchase to completely fill out the form.

Sometimes long capture forms can be a good choice, such as when your intention is to screen out people who are only casually interested in buying. (Unfortunately, most businesses don't have that intent when they use the long capture form. They probably just don't know any other alternatives.) Another situation when long capture is fine to use is when it's mandatory to fill it out whether they want to or not. Tax forms are a good example of this. They are the worst forms ever, but people have to fill them out, or hire someone to do it for them. They have no choice if they want to stay within the law.

The most common reason a company may use a long capture form is to try to get as much information as possible, usually because it needs (or thinks it needs) lots of information to qualify prospects or for system requirements, background checks, and so on. This is typical in companies that have been around for a long time.

The problem is long capture forms are often not the best convert-ing type of form, especially for lead generation. Why? There are a few reasons. First of all, they overwhelm people. Humans have shorter atten-tion spans than ever before, and the thought of filling out a long form is daunting.

Second, long forms take an investment of time. People think they're busy, even if they're not. One minute they may decide they have time to contact you; then, seeing the long form, they might decide they don't have time after all. Maybe they'll save it for later. (When that happens, you can be fairly certain they'll probably never get back to it.) They might not be able to answer some of the questions on the spot; again, they will probably put it off until later and may never come back.

These are some examples of why long capture forms aren't typically the most effective information capture strategies. Despite the low con-version rates, though, online businesses continue to use these outdated forms. So what's a better solution? There are several options to choose from, depending on the situation. First, let's take a look at the simplest type web of form strategy, short capture.

Short Capture Web Forms

You've probably seen websites that say, "Sign up for my newsletter," or something to that effect, and they ask for an e-mail address and maybe a name at most. This would be one example of a common short capture form (Figure 3.3). It may not be a high converting example, but it technically qualifies because of how few fields it requires.

Short capture forms are becoming more and more popular. For all the reasons long capture doesn't work, short capture most often does. It doesn't take a long time, it's not overwhelming, and there aren't a lot of complicated questions. These forms usually have one to six fields.

Generally, people aren't going to fill out your form just because you want them to. These days, people are very selective about what messages and companies they allow into their inboxes. You need to entice them to fill out the form by making some sort of highly desirable, relevant, free, or low-cost offer to give them in return. The better your offer, the more information they'll be willing to give you. This is the key to getting lots of people filling out your forms.

Sign Up

It's free and anyone can join

First Name

Your E-mail

Sign Up

Figure 3.3 **Short capture forms have become popular because they can be less daunting, fast to fill out, and therefore convert better than long capture forms.**

How do you know what that offer should be? How many is the perfect number of fields? You figure that out by first defining what I call the Ideal Conversion Point (ICP).

How to Find the Ideal Conversion Point With the right offer associated with your forms, you will have higher conversions and you will be able to ask for more information than just their name and e-mail. For example, if I offered a $100,000 sports car with no strings attached (assuming visitors believed it was a legitimate offer), how much personal information do you think they would be willing to give me in exchange? They'd probably tell me anything I wanted to know, right?

Now, it's not really practical to give away an expensive item like that in real life, right? But a more reasonable offer is usually something that doesn't cost you much (or anything) but is still tangible and valuable to the visitor. E-books, free reports, videos, and tutorials are all popular options. Defining the ICP helps you figure out what the topic of the offer should be. Figure 3.4 is a diagram I find helpful when explaining this concept.

There are two important pieces to the ICP: the visitors' true desire (what they *really* want from you) and your true desire (what you *really* want from them). The actual ICP is the point where both parties get what

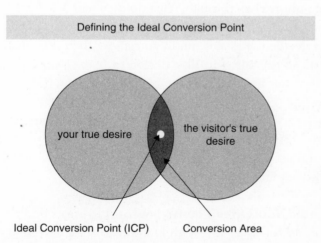

Figure 3.4 The Ideal Conversion Point is the theoretical point at which the ideal conversion exchange is made. Once you've defined the Ideal Conversion Point, you can begin to design a conversion path that gets as close as possible to that point.

they truly desire. These are never going to be the same desire because you want something totally different from what they want; you are on opposite sides of the information exchange. The ICP is a hypothetical place, almost impossible to reach, but you want to get as close to it as possible. Fortunately, there is some overlap where you're both close enough to your true desires that a conversion happens, and there's an exchange of information. This conversion area is marked by the darker shaded area in the diagram. The closer you get to the center of the overlap, the closer you are to the ICP, and the more information you can request without majorly affecting conversion rates.

How do you identify the exact ICP? It's all about true desire; that's the key. Start by asking yourself the following questions:

- What do you desire from visitors?
- What do visitors desire from you?
- How can you give them what they desire?

Let's say you run a pet supply company and you offer cat toys as one of your product lines. Let's also say you drive traffic to your website with advertising on Google. People searching for *cat toys* online see your ad on Google and click it to get to your website.

When visitors click through, what do they see? Maybe they see your home page, possibly a shopping catalog, or maybe a category page about cats. If you decide the goal is simply to capture their information before trying to make the sale, you may decide to make a separate page with nothing on it but an offer and the opt-in web form. (These are called landing pages.) What offer will they see? I've often encountered landing pages that have an offer that says something such as, "Sign up for more information." But that's not really a tangible offer, and it's not very enticing. Let's define this ICP together to figure out what else they could offer on this landing page.

What Should You Offer Them?   What do visitors desire when they click on an ad for a cat toy? Think about that for a second. If they're searching for the keywords *cat toy*, what do they really desire?

Well, a cat toy, right?

So, if we offered them a cat toy for free on the landing page, they would convert, right?

That's the answer I get most often when I ask people this question, but that's not really the *true* desire.

Let's dig a little deeper. What do visitors *truly desire*? Do they truly desire a cat toy, or is that just what they're looking for?

To find out their true desire, you have to ask another question. *Why* do they want a cat toy? Or more specifically, why did they search for *cat toy* on Google?

Most likely it's to make their cat happy, right? (Or someone else's cat, in the case of gift buying, but let's keep this simple for now.) The toy is just the means to get there. Is that the true desire—making their cat happy? We're getting there, but we're not there yet. Keep digging. Why do the visitors want their cat to be happy?

What visitors truly desire is to make *themselves* happy by seeing that their cat is happy and well cared for. There. We made it. That's the true desire. Visitors want to feel good by making their cat happy.

Can you give them that? Maybe, maybe not. Remember, I said the ICP is a place that's almost impossible, and not feasible, to reach in reality. But knowing the visitor's true desire is your first step in designing a truly enticing offer. The closer you can get to it, the more conversions you'll have and the more questions you can ask.

Let's leave that for now, and look at what you, the business owner, truly desire from the visitors. At the end of the day, you want them to buy something. Before we get there, though, you desire that they get through this one microconversion of giving you their information. So, what do you want at *this* point on this landing page? You want as much information from them as possible, right? In an ideal world, you'd want to know *everything* about them.

People often ask me how I get so many conversions while asking for so much information on my web forms. After all, conversion rate best practices generally say you should ask for as little information as possible on the form. This makes sense for getting conversions at this point, but having that extra bit of information can mean huge boosts in the conversion rates farther down the funnel. It's worth taking some time to figure out the most enticing offer so that you can capture more information.

The closer you get to the vistors' true desire in what you're offering, the more information they will give you through the web form.

So, if you could give away the coolest cat toy ever, a $40 value, guaranteed to make the cat happy, with free shipping, and no catch or strings attached—that's pretty close to their true desire. How many fields do you think your visitors will fill out in exchange for that? I can tell you from experience that it's almost unlimited. In return for that much value, they're going to give you just about anything you want to ask for in that web form. They might even give you their Social Security number if you ask for it.

Now, giving away that much may not be a practical expense for you. But that's okay because you don't really need their Social Security number or anything even close to that much personal information. You're aiming for someplace *near* the ICP, someplace in the overlap conversion area of Figure 3.4. What can you give people that's close enough to their true desire (the feeling of happiness they get from seeing their cat happy) for them to give you more information than just their name and e-mail?

We know from our analysis that they want a cat toy to make themselves happy as they watch their cat being happy. It's probably not feasible in terms of cost vs. benefit to give everyone who comes to the page a free toy, but you do want to give away something that comes close to what his or her true desire is, preferably something that's free (or close to free) and easy for you to deliver. A popular option is free information. But as I mentioned before, "Fill out this form for more information" is often just not enticing enough to yield high conversions.

Let's say you want to offer a free report. What would that report be about? I can tell you from experience that a good title might be something like *The 7 Coolest Cat Toys of All Time—Guaranteed to Put a Smile on Your Cat's Face*. That's pretty close. Just reading the title, visitors can picture their cat happily playing with one of the toys. This, in turn, puts a smile on their faces. Bingo! Happy cat. Happy visitors. It also covers what they're looking for when they click that ad on Google—buying a cat toy. You're giving them information about what they're looking for, as well as what they truly desire.

When you get that close to their true desire, they will gladly tell you things such as their first name, last name, e-mail address, phone number, how many cats they have, how often they buy cat toys, and maybe even a few other interesting things, such as whether they also have dogs. (Remember, you run a pet supply company, not just a cat toy company. Knowing whether they have dogs can help you sell dog-related items down the road.) Now you're thinking with a customer-centric mind-set, and from a holistic perspective.

Why and When You Shouldn't Just Give Away Free Products
Why wouldn't we just give away free samples if they convert so well? Well, you can, especially if the profit margin makes sense, but there's one thing to keep in mind. Yes, you'll get the opt-in pretty often (as long as you're reaching the true desire), but you may be filling your database with people who aren't really good prospects or buyers. You're essentially giving away product to your suspects who will most likely never buy. So your return on investment (ROI) can go down. There are many people out there who just surf around looking for free stuff. They're not really prospects because they have no intention of buying anything ever. You build a nice big list and this microconversion goes up, but your bottom line conversion rate suffers. You might want to save your free samples for people who are qualified and farther along in your funnel. Then the ROI is better.

There are ways to make free samples work, especially if you have a brick-and-mortar store. For example, you can give away a *coupon* for free samples. But visitors have to come into the store to redeem it. Once they are in the store, it's more likely you'll convert them to a customer on the spot. This is a great example of online to off-line marketing. You capture their information in exchange for the coupon, but the coupon is only worth something if they come into the store. Even if they don't come into the store right away, you still have their e-mail address and can keep marketing to them.

Giving away a free product works so well in traditional marketing because it's tangible and valuable. Information, such as "seven cool cat toys," is valuable too, but it's not tangible until you put it into some physical form. By calling it an e-book or a report, you turn mere information and ideas into a tangible thing. You can help make the report appear even more tangible with graphics, such as a well-designed, 3-D art cover that makes it look like an actual tangible item.

How to Use The Get Principle When Designing Your Offers
Once you have a good information capture offer figured out, you still have to present it to visitors in an appealing way to get the conversion. You'd be surprised how many people have really valuable information in their offer but still say, "Sign up for more information" in the headline or description. Signing up for more information is often outside or floating on the borderline of the conversion area overlap on the ICP diagram. Signing up is what *you* truly desire from them, but more information is

not what *they* truly desire from you. They won't usually find the idea of "more information" enticing enough to make the exchange. Every offer is a sales pitch, even the free ones, so pay special attention to the words you use in the headlines where you're pitching your offers.

People often ask me how to present their offer on the page. It can be challenging to create an enticing headline that shows the true value, so I created *The Get principle* to make it easy. When you're not sure what to say, start with the word *get* in your headline, and then add on what the offer is. When you start this way, you'll be headed in the right direction. You'll probably want to refine the headline a little, but it's a great start. Here are a couple of examples:

- *Get* a coupon for 50% off our best-selling cat toys.
- *Get* our free guide: *Seven Coolest Cat Toys.*

With the word "get," you're using active language from a customer-centric perspective. It's why they're coming to the website in the first place—to *get* something. You don't have to spend hours working out the perfect headline. ***Visitors just want to get something; just give them what they want, and tell them what they're going to get***. You don't have to literally use the word *get*, but it's a great way to start brainstorming from a customer-centric perspective.

The ICP concept is one secret to my success with increasing conversion rates using information capture. The other secret is designing smarter web forms. Let's take a closer look at that right now.

How to Build a Short Capture Form　Short forms can be anywhere from one to six fields, typically. The exact number is up to you, but it should be the minimum amount of information you need to follow up. The number of fields should keep conversions in mind and be based on what you learned about your visitors' ICP. After all, you can always send an e-mail to gather more information later, after you've had time to establish your credibility and gain some level of trust.

More and more businesses are using short capture forms these days. Common field combinations include first name, last name, phone, and e-mail. They may also include fields such as company or website URL. The most popular, though, is a form that asks only for first name and e-mail or just an e-mail address. That first name is powerful, though, because e-mail marketing systems let you merge the first name into e-mails to make the message more customer-centric. This personalization can lead to higher open rates and click rates, and ultimately higher conversion rates down the line.

Short-to-Long Capture Variation

This type of web form is one of the innovations I discovered early in my career as a conversion consultant. It's a way to get the benefits of long forms, without losing the leads that don't have time or are overwhelmed. Long capture forms were too long, so people didn't fill them out. But they did collect lots of good information. Short capture forms had better conversion rates but didn't always collect enough information to make the sale in the long run, so we combined the two. A short capture form is used as the first step in the process. Then when visitors click the Submit button, they are taken to a second, longer form. On this longer form, any information already provided is prefilled if possible.

This did increase conversions, but it frustrated some people, especially if they believed the first form was the only form to fill out. We didn't feel comfortable with this, so the form evolved to the next level: the multistep form type.

However, conversion rates for short-to-long capture were still high, and there are times when this is still a good technique. Overall, I have seen that going from just a long capture to adding a short capture step before it, we were increasing lead generation from the short form two to three times what the long capture forms had alone. You have to decide whether the few people who get frustrated are worth sacrificing for better conversions. Sometimes my answer has been yes; sometimes, no.

Multistep Web Forms

A multistep capture is where you take one long form and break it up into a series of steps. The visitor moves from one step to the next, and you never ask the same question more than once. You basically take the long form and chop it up to make it less overwhelming (Figure 3.5).

Shopping carts are evolving to the multistep model because the conversions can be so much higher. Many e-commerce forms contain lots

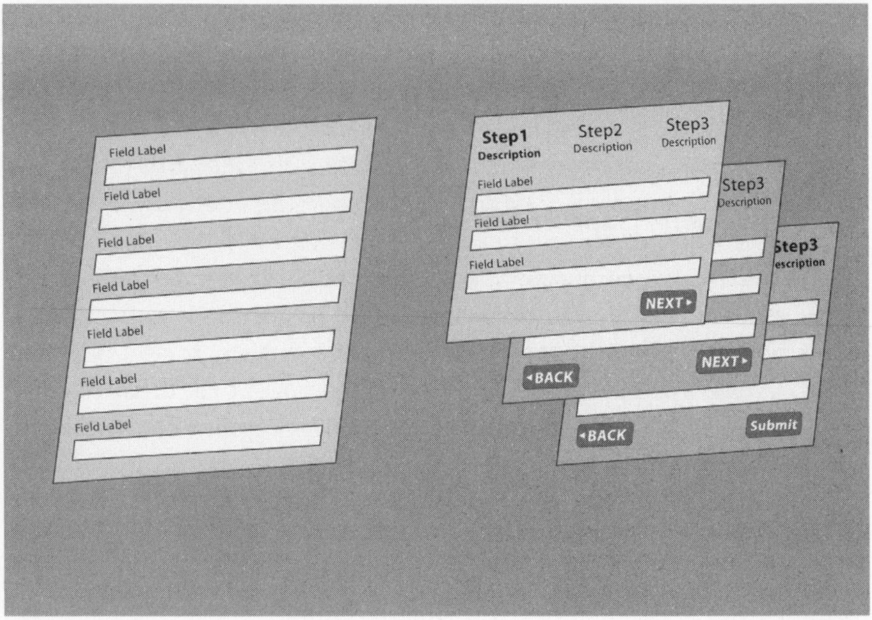

Figure 3.5 Multistep forms help people move through the process faster. Step indicators let people know where they are in the process of filling out the form, and how far they have to go.

of information to fill out on one page, so this is one place where a multi-step form can ease the pain of long capture. Shorter forms are just easier to fill out and less overwhelming.

There are lots of fancy ways to design a multistep form, such as accordion checkouts, tab-based forms, and so on. Generally, though, you're simply breaking up a long capture form into multiple steps.

Using Step Indicators to Keep People Moving Forward
Depending on your products and offerings, you may have many steps in your multistep checkout process. For example, the steps on a shopping cart page might be contact information → billing information → shipping information → credit card details → confirmation. In this case, it might a good idea to use step indicators listed as *step 2* or *part 4 of 5* so that people know how far along they are in the process (see Figure 3.5). Step indicators show customers where they are and where they're going.

It's important to know that certain kinds of multistep checkouts can actually *reduce* conversion rates. Have you ever been ready to pay for an item online, and the website forces you to register or create an account before you can check out? The logic behind this makes some sense—the business wants to keep the information on file for future purchases. But it can be a dangerous move in terms of conversions. People sometimes resent being forced to create an account when all they want to do is pay for an item and leave. That's why adding a guest checkout option has become very popular, and I highly recommend it.

Of course, every business is different. It's important to test which type of form or checkout works best for your website. You're going to learn how to do this in the next chapter on split testing.

Smooth Capture Web Forms

An even more evolved series of techniques for multistep web forms is what I call smooth capture. I solidified the smooth capture strategy around 2005 and have been using it with my clients secretly ever since. I've been surprised that more websites haven't used this strategy before now. I'm noticing other companies just starting to use similar strategies, though, so I won't be surprised if these techniques soon become more common practice.

Smooth capture uses a lot of moving parts and theories, and you need to understand some other concepts first. So we're going to cover it in more detail at the end of this book in the advanced strategies chapter. For now, just realize that you don't have to settle for weaker web forms. There are ways to increase conversions *and* capture lots of juicy details about your prospects. Compared with smooth capture forms, basic multistep web forms are ancient history for myself and my clients.

Common Mistakes to Avoid with Information Capture

- *Don't ask for just a name without splitting it up into first name and last name.* If you ask for just a name, people will sometimes use their first name, sometimes their full name, and sometimes even a nickname. When using a name merge field in your e-mail marketing, you can accidentally start your e-mail with "Dear Jane Smith," when you meant to say "Dear Jane." Asking for someone's full name can

sometimes hurt conversions because that information is more personal. There's more anonymity with just a first name. Also, using
the first name merge feature in your e-mails can lift open rates by
making them more personal and customer-centric. So, if you have
a choice, ask for first name only or first and last names in separate
fields. Yes, there are ways to split a full name into first and last using
code, but it doesn't come without its flaws.

- *Don't forget to ask for an e-mail address.* Some businesses shy away from
  asking for an e-mail address because they're afraid people will only
  give them fake addresses or because they don't use e-mail marketing.
  But e-mail is a standard method of communication in the modern
  world, and it's still one of the most valuable pieces of information
  you can get. If you are winding up with a lot of fake e-mail addresses,
  you might want to raise the value of your offer or consider another
  method of verifying the e-mail before you deliver the offer, such as
  a confirmation or e-mail opt-in provided by your e-mail marketing
  company.

- *Don't be afraid to ask for their phone number.* People have often told
  me they don't want a phone field in their short capture forms because
  they think people will be discouraged from filling out the form. But
  in tests, I've found the phone field rarely scares people away, as long as
  it's marked as optional. In fact, most people will give you their phone
  number without a concern. Sometimes they will also give a fake or
  bad phone number, but is that really such a bad thing? I've also found
  through experience that the people who guard their phone numbers
  often aren't the best prospects anyway. Adding a phone number field
  might cause a minor dip in conversions, but that is negligible compared with the value of getting a phone number, if you actually plan
  to use it. When you actually take the time to call and chat with people
  personally, you may be surprised how happy they are that you reached
  out. The world is full of anonymous phone scripts, telemarketers, and
  automated marketing. When you take the time to pick up the phone
  and actually talk to someone, that person often really appreciates it. And
  of course, with the increase of text messaging (SMS), this can also prove
  valuable if used strategically.

- *Don't forget to differentiate between phone and cell phone fields.* If you plan
  to do text message marketing, be sure to ask for mobile phone or cell
  phone in the correct field. If you ask for them separately, you have

the ability to market via text message. If you simply ask for phone, they may give you a landline by default. This is especially important if you market to the younger generations. As we move toward wider adoption of smartphones, texting is becoming standard. Also, make sure to ask for the *best* number to contact visitors. It sounds odd, but they may not realize you actually want to talk to them on the phone. They may think you want the number for something else.

- *Don't add too many questions and fields on one screen.* Don't use long capture forms without a good reason. Sometimes they can convert better than multistep or short forms, but it's rare. If you think you have a good reason to use a long capture form, set up a simple split test to see if your hunch is correct. Don't guess; let the data tell you. Don't worry; we'll go into split testing in detail in the next chapter.

- *Don't include an offer that doesn't attempt to reach the ICP.* "Fill out this form for more information" is not a valuable tangible offer; neither is "Learn more" or "Sign up for our newsletter." These days, for information capture to work well, you need an equal exchange of value for information. You have to give to get. Give visitors something they truly value that comes as close as possible to the ICP. Reports, e-books, tutorials, video series, discounts, and free samples are all valuable options. Just be sure you use an enticing headline. When in doubt, use The Get principle to help. You can use The Get principle in the call to action and Submit buttons, too.

- *Don't offer something just to offer something.* Making an irrelevant offer is almost as bad as making a low-value offer. Most likely, it will only waste valuable real estate on your page. To provide the best value and get the most conversions possible, you should match visitors' true desire as closely as possible.

- *Don't use "free" too liberally.* I once had a client who gave away a physical product for free, including free shipping. It was a great value, so he had a conversion rate exceeding 30 percent on his traffic (which is good). But he wound up attracting the wrong kind of customer (freebie seekers, aka "suspects") and lowered his bottom line conversion rate at the end of the day. He might have done better offering a discount coupon or free report instead. Free giveaways can work, but be careful of the user context (setting and intentions) of the traffic you're sending to the offer.

- *Don't forget to use a secure page when asking for personal information.* Any time you ask for personal information, such as mailing or billing addresses, credit cards, and the like, make sure you have a secure page. People are used to looking for that now. It's a simple feature to implement, and it's your duty to your customers to protect their personal information.

- *Don't assume your visitor is unwilling to give you more information.* You never know how much information someone might give you unless you ask. Maybe a multistep form, a short-to-long form, or even a smooth capture would work well in your situation. Remember, the closer your offer is to his or her true desire and the ICP, the more information you can ask for. There's only one way to know for sure, and that's by split testing it.

Build Your Skills

The skills lab for this chapter will help you come up with enticing, valuable offers and show you how to build a web form in just a few minutes.

You can find this skills lab at www.ConvertEveryClick.com/ chapter3

CHAPTER FOUR

Split-Testing Strategies

Do you remember when blind taste tests were the popular format for TV commercials? Probably the most famous was the Pepsi Challenge, but there were blind tests for Mexican beers, ketchups, and even chocolate chip cookie dough. You also sometimes see blind smell tests for perfumes and blind touch tests for fabric softeners. A more recent example of a blind test is the Bing It On test, where Bing faces off against Google.

My dad used this same technique when I was a kid to convince me that yellow American cheese tastes the same as white American cheese. I was a relatively picky eater and didn't like yellow cheese at all. I'm a fairly visual person, so for me the way a food *looks* affects how it tastes. My dad got really frustrated when I wouldn't eat the yellow cheese, so he made me two sandwiches and had me try them with a blindfold on. I really couldn't tell the difference. I was vindicated later, though, when he tried to trick me by putting fat-free cream cheese into the regular cream cheese container. I could tell the difference right away!

The concept of split testing in marketing may have originated with blind tests, but modern technology on the Internet has made the idea of split testing much simpler, more achievable, and much more valuable for businesses. A split test today is a little different from a straight blind test, but they both originated from the scientific method. In the cheese example, I knew I was being tested. The user context was different than a real-life experience would be (like with the cream cheese). With a true split test, we have the ability to test a large pool of people who don't even know they're being tested. This increases accuracy dramatically.

The other difference relates to the overall goal of the test. With the exception of scientific studies, the blind test examples like the Pepsi Challenge are generally used for marketing purposes. The goal is to open people's minds to the option of switching brands. A brand is only going to show you a blind test if they *know* it will favor them. Split tests are used to gather data on which design or element is *actually* more popular. Our goal with a split test online is to find out which design or style is better, and by exactly how much, so that we can strategically improve the site.

You can split test many different things. In my conversion rate optimization company, we split test web page designs, traffic (like Google ads), e-mail subject lines, and more. For PPC ads, the conversion may be measured by click tracking or even on-page conversions. For e-mail testing, the conversion measurement is usually the open rate or click-through rate. For anything on a web page, we define the conversion point, which can be something like a click, an opt-in, a purchase, and so on as we discussed in Chapter 1. Because of split-testing software, we get more accurate data regarding the actual conversion rates and we can optimize to get closer to converting every click.

Here's How It Works

Let's say you redesigned one of the pages on your website and you think it will lift conversions. No matter how good the new page is, you'll still want to test it to be sure it's better than the old one. You set up a split test with the new version of the page going against the old version. You load the URLs for both versions into the special testing software and run the test. Figure 4.1 shows you how this looks. You'd be surprised how many people just replace their page without running a split test and wind up hurting their conversions.

Let's say you have 1,000 visitors coming to that page over a period of time. If you have two versions of the page, the software automatically splits the traffic and sends 500 people to one page and 500 to the other. You set a conversion goal you want to measure (such as a sale), and then the software keeps track of how many visitors convert on each page.

All of this happens automatically, so all you need to do is watch and wait to see which version wins. Most split-testing software will help you decide when you have enough data to declare a winner. Then you make that version your live page online. Sometimes getting a clear winner can take a long time (I've seen as long as two months for a small

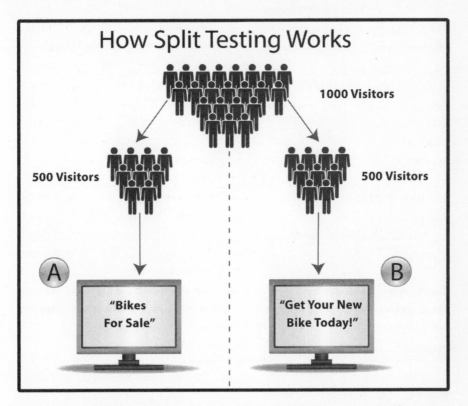

How Split Testing Works

1000 Visitors

500 Visitors

500 Visitors

A

B

"Bikes For Sale"

"Get Your New Bike Today!"

Figure 4.1 Split testing is the strategy of splitting your traffic up so you can send some people to your current web page and some to your new idea to see which gets better results. This allows you to measure real behavior instead of making assumptions or guessing.

website). Sometimes it happens in a matter of minutes, for websites with thousands of conversions per day. What's important to know is that you need to have enough traffic to supply meaningful numbers.

Small pools of data can provide inaccurate results. When you flip a coin, the statistical chance of it landing on heads is 50 percent. But if you flip it only four times, it might come up tails every single time. You need more data. If you flip the coin 100 times, it might come up heads 48 times and tails 52 times. Now the data shows the 50 percent statistic more closely. Having enough data is called being statistically significant.

This concept is really important when split testing your web pages. Just like the coin flip, version A of a web page might have 10 conversions in a row, and you might assume it's the winner and quit there. But if

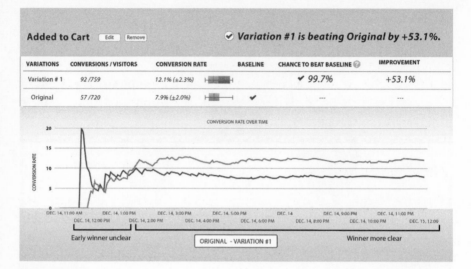

Figure 4.2 In order to be confident that the results of a split test are valid, you need statistical significance. Statistical significance is the scientific measurement of confidence in an outcome.

you left the test running longer and collected more data, you might find out that over time version B is actually the winner. You need to collect enough data. Fortunately, most software will help you figure out when you have enough. You need to collect more data to reach what statisticians call statistical significance, which is a measurement of the mathematical confidence that one variation is better than another. The general rule of thumb in statistics is that you want a 95 percent level of confidence or more. I personally shoot for 98 percent or above, if possible, but there are other factors I look for as well, which we'll talk about later. Figure 4.2 shows how early winners can be proven wrong in the long run.

Split testing can get really addictive. Once you have a clear winner, you can get to work building something else that might beat it. It's a continual process of improvement that uses statistical data to back up your decisions. This is the real reason conversion rate optimization works so well: everything gets tested and tracked.

Traditional conversion rate optimization primarily looks at on-page split testing for websites, so that's what we're going to focus on for now. Once you understand the concept of split testing, though, you can use it to test your e-mail marketing, pay-per-click ads—pretty much anything you want. You may have to design some creative ways of testing these other things or use different software, but the concept is still the same.

What Is A/B Testing?

A/B testing just means there are two choices: A and B. You could have two different headlines on your home page, and you want to test to know which one converts better. It may seem silly to call it A/B instead of just a split test, but there are other, more complicated, split tests you can run. We'll get to those shortly.

How and When to Use A/B Testing

There are a couple of ways to perform an A/B split test on a web page. You can have two versions of the page hosted on separate URLs (website addresses like www.yoursite.com) and enter the URLs into free testing software like Google Content Experiments. Another option is to use paid software, such as Optimizely or Visual Website Optimizer, which gives you a visual editor to use. With these, you enter the URL for the current live page and make changes directly in the testing software, using the drag-and-drop visual editor. This option is good for small changes. For large or complicated changes, it's often easier to host different URLs.

The visual editor is great if you don't have a web design team in-house and have to do everything yourself. You don't need to know anything about code. You just make the changes using the visual editor, and the software automatically codes the changes onto a special test page. For smaller websites and companies, this is a great way to get started split testing sooner.

You may be wondering how big the tests should be. Should you test one small idea at a time, like changing a headline or image, or test big sweeping changes like testing a completely new page layout? I'd say it depends on your goals and experience. If you test many changes at once, you can make great strides in a short amount of time. However, it can be difficult to tell which change had the desired effect. On the other hand, it can take longer to make meaningful gains if you're testing one thing at a time, but it will be easier to understand what each change is doing to your conversions.

Because of my experience level, my preference is usually to make larger, more complicated changes as soon as possible. But even I like to start with smaller changes first to confirm that our assumptions are correct before taking big risks. As a novice, you may want to start smaller and test one or two changes at a time. The more traffic and sales you have, the more a small change will make a big difference. With my biggest clients, we usually discuss the strategy options and decide together which is the best course of action for each client's unique situation.

When You Should Test

A/B testing should be used anytime you're implementing a new idea or change to a web page where conversions online matter to you. One of the largest pitfalls with conversion is that someone will have an idea, but the implementation of that idea will have a fatal flaw. I see far more implementation problems than bad ideas. For example, you might have the idea to change the look of a web page, but your new design has the Buy Now button too far down the page. The idea for the new look isn't bad, but the implementation of positioning the Buy Now button ends up being the fatal flaw. The first step is to find out that it has a fatal flaw. You find that out with a test.

One of the biggest failures I've ever seen happened because a new website wasn't tested against the old one. We're talking about a real multi-million-dollar business in this example. They were completely obsessed with rebranding their website and company. They did usability studies and made the new site pretty and modern with all the bells and whistles the designer could think up. From a visual standpoint, it was gorgeous.

But they didn't test the old website against the new website.

Their sales plummeted over 300 percent for months, and it took many more months to recover. Visitors simply couldn't find the right pages or the right information to make the purchase. This one failure cost them millions of dollars in lost revenue, and they could have fixed it very quickly with a simple A/B split test.

So raise your right hand and repeat after me: *No matter how smart or strategic I am, I realize there's always a chance a change will make conversions worse. I solemnly swear I will seriously consider split testing my new web pages against the old ones to make sure I don't mess anything up.*

Good. Now we can move on.

What Is Multivariate Testing?

A test with more than two versions or variables, as opposed to just the two in an A/B test, is called a multivariate test. Technically, all split tests are multivariate tests, because *multi* really means two or more. But in the conversion world, we use the word *multivariate* to mean "more than two."

There are several types of multivariate testing. The first one is what we call an A/B/C/D test, or an A/B/n. An A/B/C/D test is really an

A/B/n test with four pages, each testing something unique. You're testing all pages against one another equally at the same time.

Let's say you have a landing page, and you're not sure how to improve conversions. So you hire four separate designers to design the same page, and then you put those pages up against one another in the testing software. In this case, you have an A/B/C/D/E test, which is not so different from the A/B test we talked about earlier. There's nothing complicated about it; there are just three extra versions of the page. The "A" is the original page, known here as the control, and B/C/D/E are the new designs.

Four is not a magic number here. You can run any number of pages against each other. It could be A/B/C/D/E, A/B/C/D/E/F, and so on. You get the point. Figure 4.3 shows a multivariate test with four versions plus the current page as a control.

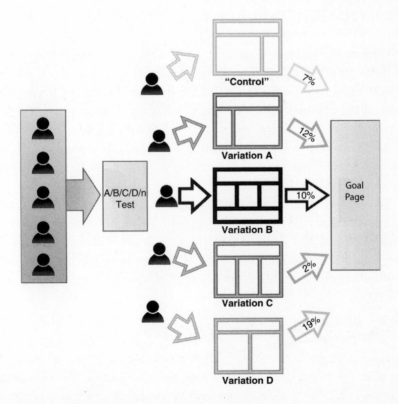

Figure 4.3 Multivariate testing allows you to split test more than just your current web page and one other version. Multivariate means testing more than two variables.

Multivariate Combo Testing

Another type of multivariate testing is what most people think of when they hear the phrase. I call this type a multivariate combo test. Let's say you have a website, and you have five different elements you want to test—a header image, a headline, two different locations for the call to action, and a sidebar callout. You could test each of those elements separately using an A/B/n test, but that would only tell you which one does better than the other. It can't tell you anything about *combinations* of those elements. A combo test lets you test all or some of the different variations in combination.

Here's an example:

Idea 1: Changing the text in the headline
Idea 2: Moving a button to the left
Idea 3: Changing the background color

With three different elements, you get many combinations. Do you test them all at once together? What if two of the ideas work and one doesn't? How would you know which one isn't working? If you combined all the changes onto one page and ran a regular A/B test against the original version of the page, how would you know what's happening? If it fails, you won't know why. If it succeeds, you won't know why. If two ideas are great and one is bad, do they cancel each other out? Will they minimize your success rate?

To create a combo test, you're going to pair up the different ideas into combined sets. We can label the original headline, button, and background color as A, C, and E. Then label the *new* headline, button, and background color as B, D, and F. Now we can start pairing them up. A combination chart might begin to look like this:

A C E   B C E
A C F   B C F
A D E   B D E
A D F   etc.

As you can see, this can get pretty confusing. It's a lot to think about. Fortunately, there is software out there to figure all this out for you.

How and When to Use Combo Testing Multivariate Combo testing has one big downfall. It needs huge amounts of traffic or will take a long time. If you're a bigger company like some of my larger clients, or if you have more than 1,000 visits a day, it's not very difficult to reach the number of people you need to build statistical significance and confidence that the test results are accurate.

But what if you have only 100 visitors a day, and you consider nine or more different variations of your test? Remember, your traffic is split evenly among all the variations of your page. So splitting that hundred people across eight variations means your data is going to take a long time to build up to statistical significance. In other words, you're going to be waiting a long time for a winner, because only nine or so people will visit each version of the page each day. Those nine people could have had a bad day. There's not really going to be enough data to give you the percentages that you need to determine a true winning combination. So, if you don't have a lot of regular traffic to your website, you should expect to leave combo tests running for many weeks or months.

You can shorten the test time a bit by using your experience and logic to rule out combinations that seem repetitive or least likely to win. Narrowing the choices lowers the number of combinations and can speed up the test. Generally, though, combo tests are best suited to companies or websites with a significant amount of traffic. If you have less traffic, you're probably better off identifying small areas you can improve and using a faster A/B split test.

So, if you're getting lots of traffic to your site, the great thing about combo testing is you can find out the best combination of elements to use to improve conversions. You'll also gain some extra confidence because if you run the test long enough, you'll see a clean curve, with the combinations that work the best at the top, tapering down a nice smooth curve to the ones that will work the worst or won't work at all. When all the results are mapped together, the curve becomes very clear. Figures 4.4, 4.5, and 4.6 all depict different ways of showing this smooth curve.

The figures show conflicting results early on, but eventually the winner emerges.

Multidimensional Testing

Another type of multivariate testing uses strategies similar to or based on Taguchi's methods. I call these multidimensional testing methods because

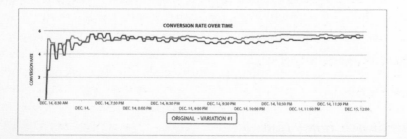

Figure 4.4 In the split-testing software programs that exist, there are different types of graphs you can view to make sure your curve is smooth before making your conclusions.

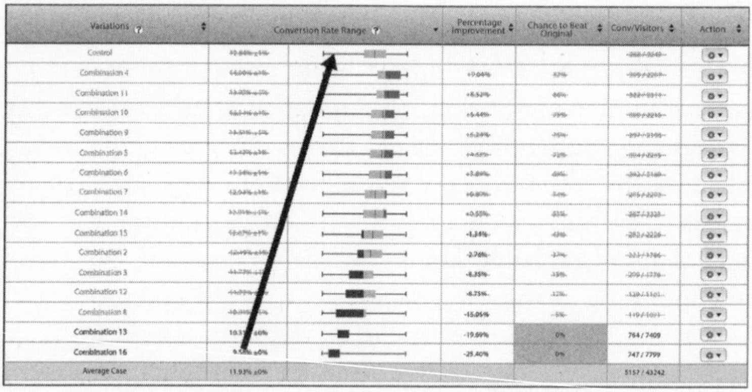

Figure 4.5 Figures 4.4 and 4.5 illustrate two such graphs.

Figure 4.6 As you can see in this graph, this particular split test started out unclear, but over time the lines separated and the winner became clearer as statistical significance was reached.

they have an extra layer of complexity. These are used to minimize the length of time you need tests to run to get the statistical significance and confidence level that you want. These methods allow you to test large numbers of variables without necessarily having a proportionately large pool of visitors to test. Unfortunately, my favorite split-testing tools have not adopted these advanced concepts yet. In the Skills Lab for this chapter, I go more in depth on this topic, exploring some of the use cases as well as breaking down the concept. Once you've mastered A/B, A/B/n, and multivariate combo tests, it will make multidimensional testing easier to learn.

The Best Testing Tools Currently Available

The secret to good split testing is in the software. You want something easy to use and reliable that provides accurate, easy-to-understand data. Although there are plenty of split-testing tools available, I do have a few favorites, which I discuss next.

Google Analytics Content Experiments

For years, one of the most common split-testing tools was Google Website Optimizer, which has since been integrated into Google Analytics. It's now called Google Analytics Content Experiments. The reason this software is so popular is that Google Analytics is such a widely used product but more so, it's free. When you combine the power of split testing with the data available inside Google Analytics, suddenly there's a whole host of conclusions you can draw and opportunities to improve conversion rates. Content Experiments is not my favorite because it's still relatively new, but it's a good place to start if you need free software. My hope is it will evolve to offer more features. Knowing Google, it's possible. Figure 4.7 shows an example of the Google Analytics Content Experiments reporting screen.

Visual Website Optimizer

Visual Website Optimizer (Figure 4.8) is another good piece of software. The company has been working in the conversion space for a while and has continually improved the software so that now it's very fast and easy to use.

Many visually inclined users like this software because they don't need to know any HTML or coding to do their own split testing. You

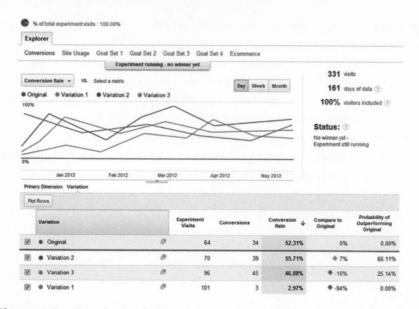

Figure 4.7 Google Analytics Content Experiments is a good tool to start with mostly because it covers the basics of A/B split testing and it's free. This illustration is an example of a report from an experiment that has yet to reach a clear winner.

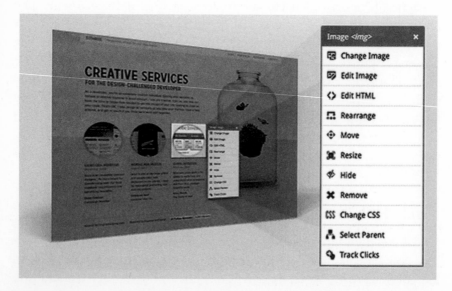

Figure 4.8 Visual Website Optimizer is a split-testing tool with many built-in features, including the ability to create your variations directly in the software with their drag-and-drop builder.

can literally click on a web page in Visual Website Optimizer, change the header, change text, and change the button—all the examples I used earlier in this chapter—without knowing anything about code. You can make things simple or complicated, but the simple ones are really easy and a great way to get your feet wet with split testing. It lets you create the variations, it splits the traffic for you, it tracks the winners and losers, and it will even tell you when it thinks you can safely declare an accurate winner. Once you make the changes you want, you can then turn on the test, run it, and never have to talk to a technology team until you know the winner. It will even automatically launch the winner for you so you don't lose any money while waiting for you to decode the winner. This is one of the major advantages of Visual Website Optimizer. It's not the only one.

I also love the qualitative data that comes from its heat map features. You can watch how people are clicking and interacting with your page and variations. I also love some of the more advanced features, such as geotargeting. All its features are wrapped into a reasonably priced bundle. That's what made Virtual Website Optimizer my favorite for a long time. It's still often my choice for small businesses.

Optimizely

Optimizely is like a shiny, newer toy for me, and it's quickly becoming my favorite tool. It's very similar to Visual Website Optimizer in its base functionality. Optimizely has a drag-and-drop editor, too, but it's built more simply, which is a good thing. Out of the box, it has fewer features. For example, you have to integrate with a third-party heat map software to use that feature. But it presents data in a more user-friendly interface. So everything that's done in Visual Website Optimizer is one step easier in Optimizely, in my opinion. At the time of this writing, Optimizely is lower priced, too. Figure 4.9 shows how Optimizely walks you through the split-testing process.

Optimizely gives great results and some really attractive displays. One of my favorite features is that it lets you watch the test results come in live, and it updates every few seconds, allowing you to watch a test like a live ticker. You can set multiple goals, such as where people click, how well they engage your website in general, or what specific paths they take. Then all these pieces of data are tracked separately but reported at once and practically in real time.

This may seem intimidating, but it's really fun. Split-testing tools are like my toys. They let me play with variations and ideas and see results.

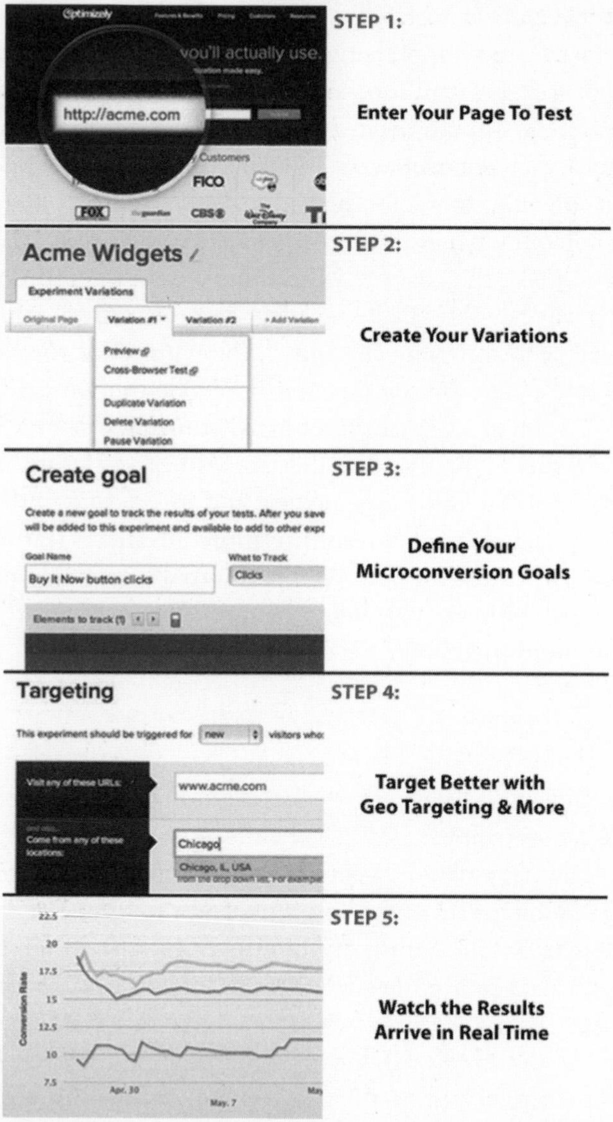
http://acme.com
STEP 1:
Enter Your Page To Test
Acme Widgets
Experiment Variations
STEP 2:
Create Your Variations
Create goal
Buy It Now button clicks
STEP 3:
Define Your
Microconversion Goals
Targeting
www.acme.com
Chicago
STEP 4:
Target Better with
Geo Targeting & More
STEP 5:
Watch the Results
Arrive in Real Time

Figure 4.9 Optimizely also makes split testing easy to do on the fly, even if you have no knowledge of coding or a dedicated IT team. While it doesn't have as many features currently as Visual Website Optimizer, it is cleaner and integrates with other important tools. At the moment, it's my favorite because of the simple user experience. But what's important if you're just getting started is that you are testing vs. not testing; even if that means using Google's free tool.

The more different ways I can see the same data, the better. Optimizely lets me create so many different types of goals easily, so I can be more holistic when looking at a microconversion point's test—it's awesome. Give yourself time to play around with this. I'll bet you're going to have fun and improve your business at the same time.

Common Mistakes to Avoid with Split Testing

- *Don't launch a new website without testing it against the old one.* You made a promise, remember? It's that important. The last thing you want to do is sabotage what you've already got going.
- *Don't assume that just because you have a good idea, you implement the idea, and you implement it well, it's going to work and convert better.* Don't get emotionally involved in your testing; the new idea might be better, or it might not be. Setting up a test in a split-testing tool takes only a few minutes and really could save you a lot of money.
- *Don't spend too much time making small, slow changes unless it's strategic.* If you're in a big business, going slow makes complete sense because a small change, even a 1 percent change in conversions, could mean a million dollars or more. But for small businesses, sometimes you're better off focusing more on the larger picture, such as fixing your funnel rather than testing a different color on your *Buy Now* button.
- *Don't forget to ensure you set up your conversion tracking correctly.* People don't like to waste their time. The worst thing in testing is to be led in the wrong direction and waste time and money. Before we do any major tests with new clients, we spend some time in the split-testing software simply testing to see if the software is interacting properly with the page and is picking up conversions accurately.
- *Don't confuse your goals.* Defining those conversion goals properly is extremely important. We might define the conversion on a page as clicking a link to buy, or we might say the conversion is getting to the success page of the actual shopping cart, meaning visitors actually bought something. But we can't forget that the bottom line conversion rate is what counts. So you want to watch how your testing goal affects your bottom line. It all depends on what data you're looking for and what you want to accomplish with it. Either way, you want to make sure the software is actually tracking appropriately before you start any serious tests. When in doubt, you can set up multiple conversion goals,

as we talked about being easy with Optimizely. You don't want to come out with incorrect data that sends you off in the wrong direction.

- *Don't let pricing scare you off.* The increase in revenue you can get from just one split test can be worth years of paying monthly software or consulting fees. On the flip side, you're also decreasing the risk of losing money from not testing. It's data that's definitely worth paying for.
- *Don't jump to conclusions when reading early test data.* Your test winners might flip-flop back and forth in the early phases of testing like you saw in Figure 4.6. One minute version A is the winner and the next, version B. To be sure, you want a clear vertical separation on the line graph between each variation's line where one is clearly the winner over the long term.
- *Don't ignore outside factors affecting the test.* Chronological issues, such as what time of day it is, what day of the week it is, or even what time of year it is can all affect data. Social media is a great example of this. If you make a post on Facebook at 10 AM on a weekday, you might get 100 likes. But if you make that same post at 6 PM on a weekend, you might get 1,000 likes (or the opposite). This is where you need to know your market really well. Are there outside factors such as seasons that might be affecting the test?

Build Your Skills

The skills lab for this chapter will show you how a split test is set up and run in the actual software.

You can find this skills lab at www.ConvertEveryClick.com/chapter4.

Hook Me Up, Benji!

Get access to a FREE 30-day trial of Optimizely and Visual Website Optimizer.
Go to www.ConvertEveryClick.com/hookmeup

CHAPTER FIVE

How to Gather Data

When we start working with a new conversion rate optimization client at my firm, we spend some time gathering data before we start making any recommendations about their website or other marketing. The holistic or big picture perspective of a business is made up of little details, which we can measure using various tools and analytics programs. By gathering data at the start, we can get closer to a complete picture of what's happening in their business and what their funnel looks like, as well as the more granular details that prove useful.

The data gathering phase brings together all the pieces that make up a business, so we can analyze what the prospects and customers are doing *before, during*, and *after* an interaction with your website or business. The more you know about what's happening in all three of those phases, the easier it is to find places to start optimizing. Generally speaking, there are two different kinds of data—quantitative and qualitative. Quantitative data includes anything that can be measured or expressed in numbers, such as how many people convert from one step to another, how many steps there are, how much traffic they have, and so on. When it comes to quantitative data, I see people commonly setting up tracking tools like Google Analytics, but data means nothing if you don't analyze it. You enter the next level of sophistication when you go beyond basic tracking and start creating intentional quantitative data through processes like split testing. Split testing qualifies as being intentional. Often some of the gems come from qualitative data, information that cannot be expressed numerically, such as where on the page people are clicking, where they're hovering, why they're coming to the page, how credible visitors think the page is, and so on. Visitor behaviors and psychology behind the page may seem relatively subjective at times, but you can still analyze and test them. When you are able to collect both kinds of data, you have a powerful foundation from which to optimize.

You will have the opportunity to optimize at all three stages. If the data shows poor traffic flow or low ROI *before* people find your website, you may want to optimize for better traffic generation. If the data shows good traffic coming in, but various microconversion points aren't performing well, you might want to optimize those pages on your website. If your upsell or referral programs aren't performing well in the *after* phase, then you may want to focus your energies on your follow-up marketing strategies. But the power is in thinking holistically.

Depending on your business and experience, you may have huge amounts of data already, or you may not have any (at least you don't think you do). Either way, it's important to get a good picture of the way things stand so that you have a baseline of assumptions to test.

Why Bother with Data Gathering?

If you are new to CRO, data gathering helps you figure out where to start with conversion rate optimization. If you are experienced, improving your data gathering mind-set and practices can help you move forward more effectively. It can show you where you might want to start testing in or on your funnel. Your ideas for improvement will come from matching up this data with your funnel and asking questions. Are people actually going where you think they are? If not, why? And how can you encourage more of them to do what you want (while still getting what they need)? What do you know about your prospects and customers? How do you know? Was it a gut instinct based on your experience, or do you have data to prove it? Is there a chance your assumptions about your customers are wrong? Isn't it possible that your prospects' and customers' desires are changing? Are they changing because of you, your industry, or the world in general? How do these changes affect their buying behavior?

These are the types of questions data gathering can answer. Data gathering is all about asking the right questions, analyzing the answers, and always asking more questions as you continue with conversion rate optimization. Data gathering doesn't stop when you start optimizing. CRO is all about learning more as you go.

Now that you know why it's important to gather data before you get started optimizing, let's look at some different strategies you can use to find the data.

Traditional Data Gathering Methods

In the days before the Internet and even today, a lot of data gathering is done with surveys, focus groups, and question-based market research. These traditional methods are still used frequently, but they each have their pros and cons, and they are no longer the only options.

Surveys are often relatively simple and inexpensive to set up, but to conduct them in a way that provides accurate results can be challenging. Surveys are designed for collecting qualitative data (perceptions of the surveyee) and converting that data into quantitative form. Surveys can provide valuable qualitative insights, but they have a number of opportunities to provide incorrect data.

First of all, the most common mistake I see is that it's easy to survey the wrong people (customers instead of prospects), which gives you skewed data. Also, the survey may ask leading questions, which means you get the answers you want to hear, rather than the real answers. The biggest problem is surveys are asking people to remember or perceive what they did in the past, and they tend to remember incorrectly. According to the psychological theory of self-perception, we humans are terrible at judging our "true selves." The way we think we behave is often incorrect when checked against observational data from things like video cameras and consumer tracking. In other words, you can't always count on the way people *think* they are. It's not a bad thing; it's just human behavior. We deceive ourselves all the time, creating imagined self-images and behaviors based on our own sets of rules and morals. Surveys can still be useful, but you have to be extra vigilant when crafting the questions and determining who you will ask to participate. But there are better ways to get reliable data you can count on.

Market research data is good for discovering generic statistics about your overall industry, your competitors, and people's perceived likelihood to switch from one company to another. It can also provide some more granular data, such as how often people visit certain websites. Getting a good lay of the land before you dive into a market is always a good idea. Some of this kind of data is available for free or a very low cost through websites such as Alexa.com.

You can also purchase more precise market research data customized for you. This is when hiring a market research firm can be useful. However, these firms are expensive to use and are really only practical for larger companies. If you are a Fortune 500–size company, it's worth considering because the data you collect could help you gain valuable market insights. Many of my clients work with companies like Nielsen Media Research, which gathers so much more data than what most people think. They have the resources to conduct custom surveys or market research for you, either by collecting new data or using their vast collections of existing data.

Trending data is another example of online market research data you can gather. Using tools such as Google and Twitter, you can see how certain keywords trend over time. This can help you determine such things as peak demand for seasonal products, which markets might be worth going into, what the search traffic is for keywords related to that market, how much it might cost to target certain people, and whether that traffic is trending up or down at certain times of the year. Trending research can help you see submarkets you might not have thought about or see whether it's worth making a separate niche website in a certain market segment based on size and opportunity potential.

Historical data is just what it sounds like—things that happened in the past: past buying behavior, past interaction with a website or an e-mail campaign, even past results from off-line marketing. You're looking for patterns, both good and bad, in the data available about past quantitative and qualitative behavior from your prospects and customers.

Generally speaking, you can find historical data from two main sources: inside your own analytics you've collected, and in outside historical information available publicly or that can be made available through purchase. Alexa.com is a good example of a source for historical data. Alexa rankings analyze web pages and show you all sorts of traffic statistics. It's great for analyzing your competition, too.

But the most valuable historical data often comes from inside your own website and other marketing. What's worked well for you in the past? What has driven prospects to buy? What has kept your prospects from buying? What data do you have access to that might help answer these questions? If you listed out all of the data you have or could retrieve, you can probably make many conclusions or at least make some assumptions that will prove valuable in your optimization efforts.

Website and Traffic Analytics

The Internet revolutionized the kind of data we are able to collect and the speed with which we can collect it. These days, we're able to gather real-time quantitative data on how website visitors *actually* behave on a website. Knowing where your traffic is coming from and what it's doing on your website are very important.

Although every business will need to collect slightly different types of data, here are some examples of important questions you should know about your website when it comes to CRO:

- How many visitors (overall and repeat) do you have?
- Are there spikes in traffic at certain times of the week, month, or year?
- Where are your visitors coming from? (Search engines? Social media? E-mail links? PPC ads?)
- Where are those people going on your website?
- What browsers are they coming from?
- How many are viewing on a mobile device? Which ones? (Phones, tablets, MP3 players, etc.)
- How long do they stay on your website?
- What pages do they look at?
- What keywords do they type into the search engines to find your website?
- Do they watch your videos? How long do they watch?
- How many people make it to your ultimate conversion point (your checkout page or an order form)?
- How many of those people actually convert?
- Are people abandoning your shopping cart at the last minute? How many?

Google Analytics should be your first resource for gathering data relating to your own website. There are lots of analytics tools on the market, but Google Analytics has become the standard that most everyone uses because it's robust and it's free.

It only takes a few minutes to install the small piece of tracking code on your website. Once the code is installed, there's a wealth of information Google can help you track about your traffic and how that traffic behaves on your website. It can also help you set goals and check your microconversion rates for certain points in your funnel. Figures 5.1 and 5.2 show just a small portion of the data you can collect using Google Analytics.

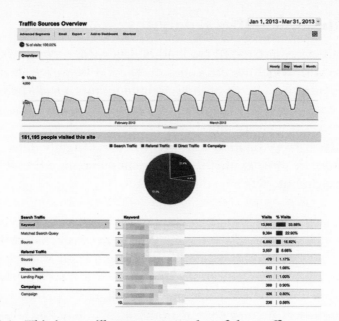

Figure 5.1   This image illustrates examples of the traffic source tracking that Google Analytics can do for you. It will even show you which keywords and phrases people are searching to find you and how often. You can use that information to optimize better. This is one of hundreds of features available for free in Google Analytics.

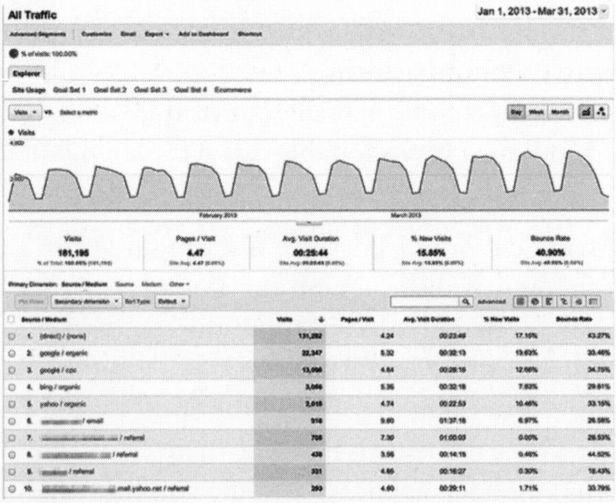

Figure 5.2   Collecting information such as how your traffic breaks down into new and repeat visitors, number of pages visited, and bounce rate helps you evaluate your website's performance over time. The data helps you know whether you're moving in the right direction.

Behavioral Analytics

One of the coolest advancements in web analytics is the ability to see what's actually happening on a website without having to spend a fortune on hardware. There's no more guessing what visitors are looking at or where they are clicking. Thanks to mouse tracking technology, we can know for sure. I like to call this behavioral analytics because we're tracking how people behave in certain circumstances.

Eye tracking is the foundation of this technology. Back in the 1800s, researchers discovered they could track which words and phrases readers' eyes stopped on and which ones they skimmed over quickly. Elite ad agencies spent significant amounts of money and waited months for results from a single test. Thankfully, that's all changed now. Studies have concluded a strong correlation between where the eye tracks on a page and clicks of a mouse. That discovery led to the development of heat map analytics (Figure 5.3). Heat maps use colors and overlays to show you the hot spots on your website, how far people are scrolling, and what they're clicking on.

Scroll tracking is another method of analyzing a web page. This data shows you visually how far down the page people are scrolling. If you know most people are only getting one-third of the way down your page, you may want to make some changes to optimize that page or at least that top third. Maybe you want to make changes that get more people to scroll farther. Maybe you want to get them to take action sooner. Or maybe one-third is just about right for your needs. No matter what you decide to do, it's great information to have at your disposal. Figure 5.4 gives you an idea of what a scroll map looks like.

Click tracking is another way to analyze a web page. Special software will show you the hot spots where people are clicking and even segment the clicks by referral source.

Let's say your data tells you that some visitors coming from an advertising campaign are clicking, but the overwhelming number of clicks are made by people coming from your e-mail list. You may decide to put more resources into optimizing your e-mail campaign (and building your list), or you may want to spend some time optimizing the campaigns that aren't working so well. Figure 5.4 shows a typical heat map based on clicks.

The hover data is important, too. If you know people hover over a certain section on your page, they're probably either reading that

Figure 5.3   On full color heat maps, the lighter events show up as varying shades of yellow, orange, red, or other colors. The different colors show you where visitors put their mice. It is an inexpensive alternative for eye tracking. While these maps are not perfect because the mouse doesn't directly represent where the eye goes, it's a great qualitative indicator of how people interact with your page.

Figure 5.4   It's important to know where people are clicking on your web page and where they're not. Perhaps people are not doing what you intended, or taking the ideal course of action. This scroll map gives you information that can help you make improvements on the page.

section or waiting for something to happen. That could be good, or it could be bad. If they're waiting for something to happen, but nothing does, maybe you need to rearrange the page or add in whatever they're expecting to happen. An example might be hovering over a product image. The visitor is probably expecting to be taken to a more detailed description of the product or a shopping page. If that's not happening, maybe it should.

This type of data is priceless when it comes to evaluating the effectiveness of a certain page and how well it's reaching your goal. Setting up good tracking tools can give you extremely valuable data.

Tools for Collecting Heat Map Data

Crazy Egg can collect great data for you, even if you don't have a lot of traffic. It's one of my favorite tools for discovering what people are really doing when they come to your website. You can find out what they're seeing, what they're not seeing, what they're clicking on, and so on. This software tracks clicks down to the individual links (something Google Analytics doesn't do). It also segments traffic sources so that you can see which traffic streams are converting better than others. And they give you reports in an easy-to-use layout, so generating new ideas is easier. Crazy Egg also has a sister company, KISSmetrics, which provides strong web analytics, A/B testing, and funnel conversion features.

ClickTale is another company I like that provides heat map data. It's a very robust system that's great for businesses of all sizes. In addition to heat maps, it offers more advanced features to help you visualize and build funnels, as well as optimize your web pages to increase bottom line conversions. ClickTale also offers web form analytics, so you can figure out where people are abandoning your forms. This data can help you decide where to split up multistep forms. ClickTale excels at providing real-time data where you can actually watch people interacting on your site.

Both Crazy Egg and ClickTale integrate smoothly with Optimizely, my favorite split-testing tool. When you use these tools together, you can gain insight into why certain split-test ideas won or lost because you can see how people interacted with each split-test variation. This insight can help you formulate more successful ideas down the line.

Test before You Test Method

For a long time, I worked on my own with CRO without really paying attention to the other people working in this relatively new field. On multiple occasions, I remember reading comments by other industry leaders stating that scenarios of 40 percent success rates on split tests were typical and to be expected. This statistic confused me because our experiences were different. We have always hovered around 90 percent success rates. Until I heard the industry statistic, I assumed our experiences were typical, which led me to carefully evaluate what we were doing differently. Our conclusion was that our data gathering strategy, which we called Test Before You Test (TBYT), was one of the largest contributors to our success rate.

Test Before You Test is the concept of using split-testing concepts to simply gather data points and confirm assumptions behind an idea before you test the actual idea. It can exponentially reduce the risk of your split tests failing. Unlike other data gathering methods like surveys and traditional market research, TBYT can be more accurate because it's conducted in real-life scenarios on actual prospects who don't know they're part of a test. In addition, to more accuracy and lower costs, you can often get your data points faster and easier.

This method is extremely powerful. In fact, this strategy can also be applied to lowering risk in environments outside of CRO, which led to my best-selling book *Failure is Obsolete*. But TBYT can seem a bit confusing and may take some practice. Learn more about how it can improve your split-testing success rate in the Skills Lab for this chapter.

Data Buying, Renting, and Modeling

I don't want to delve too deeply into buying data because it's a complex topic that could be a separate, highly technical book. But it can be a powerful way to collect a lot of data points very quickly. My company ConversionCore has access to huge amounts of demographic and psychographic data for billions of people, thanks to partnerships with other companies. Once you purchase certain information, you can use some really cool strategies, including appending and reverse appending, which let you extrapolate lots more data. Data buying, data renting, and modeling are typically only available for bigger companies who can afford to buy large amounts of data. This may or may not be right for you, but just be aware that it can be very profitable for your business.

E-mail Marketing Data

Most e-mail marketing companies offer analytics data (Figure 5.5). At the very least, you can collect data on open rates and click-through rates. Knowing how many people read your messages and which ones get more clicks will help you create more targeted, effective e-mail in the future. From a HCRO perspective, optimizing your e-mail involves optimizing where on your website they come from, and where you send them in the e-mails.

Here are some questions to ask about e-mail marketing:

- What is your open rate?
- Are people viewing on a computer or mobile device?
- How many people click links in your e-mails?
- Which links get clicked most often?
- How many unsubscribe? When do they unsubscribe?
- Where are they exiting from?
- How did they get on your list?
- What is/was their true desire?
- Where are you sending them?
- How does this e-mail play a role in your funnel? And is your funnel linear enough?

Video Analytics

If you use video in any part of your funnel (and I hope you do), video tools such as Wistia and Brightcove offer great analytics on information, such as how many people are watching your video and how far they get before they stop watching. If you know people are not watching long enough to get to your call to action, you can easily take steps to improve your video. We will discuss video in more detail in Chapter 8.

Traffic Analytics

Paying attention to traffic analytics such as Google AdWords or other pay-per-click (PPC) analytics is vital to an effective HCRO strategy.

Broadcast Stats

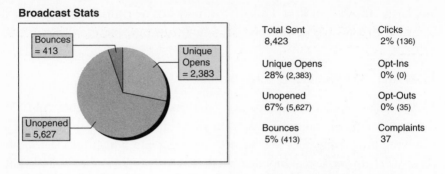

Total Sent 8,423	Clicks 2% (136)
Unique Opens 28% (2,383)	Opt-Ins 0% (0)
Unopened 67% (5,627)	Opt-Outs 0% (35)
Bounces 5% (413)	Complaints 37

Figure 5.5   The data provided by your e-mail marketing provider can give you insight into how to improve your open rates, click-through rates, and other microconversion points. Considering how these micro-conversions play a role in your overall funnel is key.

Here are some questions to get you started gathering data from your traffic sources such as PPC advertising:

- What's your click-through rate?
- What's your landing page conversion rate?
- What types of ads get clicked on most often?
- Which ad copy gets the most clicks?
- Which ad copy gets the most bottom line conversions?

It's all about optimizing your traffic for conversion. As an example, Google AdWords can track microconversions, which gives you insight into where things stand and where they can go.

One awesome tool anyone can use (even without buying a single ad) is the Google AdWords Keyword Planner (as shown in Figure 5.6, this tool was previously called the "External Keyword Tool"). With this free online software, you can find out how many people are searching for a certain keyword or phrase, and what other related keywords they are also searching for (see Figure 5.6). This keyword tool was recently integrated into the Google's Keyword Planner, which has even more features to help you design your Google ad campaigns. It will give you an idea for the average monthly searches on certain keywords, and how competitive those keywords are, which is a

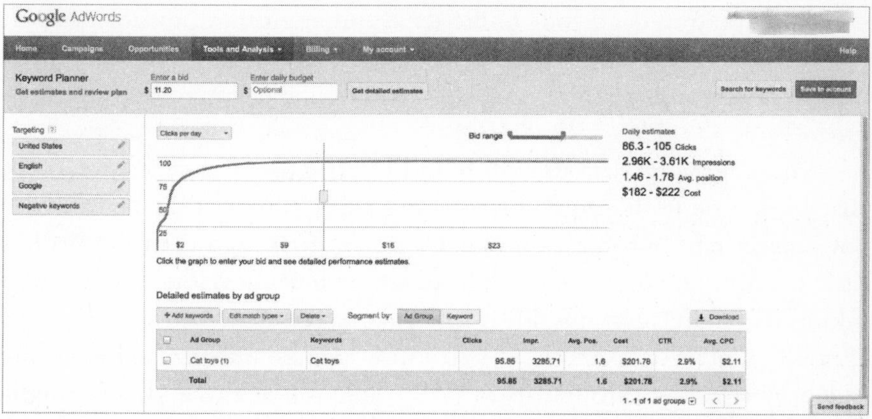

Figure 5.6 The Google AdWords Keyword Planner is a goldmine of keyword and market competition data.

key indicator for how much it will cost you to get traffic on those keywords.

Knowing the most searched for keywords in your industry and discovering businesses advertising on those keywords tells you a lot about the intentions of the searchers, which are important to consider when creating a more customer-centric experience.

There are many other sources of data including opposition research systems, phone analytics, engagement analytics, et cetera. These types are typically more advanced; however, it's good to know they exist when the time comes to implement more sophisticated strategies.

What Do You Do with All the Data?

So what's the bottom line here? It's collecting data so that you can answer certain questions, such as *Why* are people behaving a certain way? and *How* can you get them to behave the way you want? This is what the remainder of the book is about: finding ways to use the data you collect to increase your conversion rates.

You want to use the data to build pictures of the overall individual visitor's experience with your company online. You can start with your website. But to build a holistic model, you also want to review your e-mail marketing data, your traffic data, and any other metrics you can get your hands on. Once you know how your visitors experience your company, you can start to tweak that experience to improve conversion rates.

Knowing what data to collect and interpreting it correctly is a skill that takes time to develop. This learning curve is part of the reason why conversion rate optimization experts are in such high demand. With a little practice and focus, you'll start to see patterns develop. When you're asking the right questions, ideas for what to test next will start to form in your mind. For example, if you know people aren't watching your video all the way through to the call to action at the end, you might want to test putting the call to action earlier, or you might just test a shorter video.

Common Mistakes to Avoid with Data Gathering

- *Don't gather data about the wrong people.* Make sure you're not confusing your prospects and your customers. If you're trying to gather data about why people aren't converting, it doesn't make sense to look at people who did convert (only your customers). Think this through before you start interpreting your data. This is a common mistake when using surveys as a data gathering method. Take customer survey data with a grain of salt if you're trying to use it to convert more prospects.
- *Don't forget to ensure your analytics is set up properly.* I've seen people get skewed data from their analytics simply because they set it up incorrectly. When this happens, they can head down a long rabbit hole of wrong assumptions and failed or misleading split tests. Take the necessary time to make sure everything is set up and working properly.
- *Don't make assumptions based on competitors.* It's dangerous to use your competitors' websites as examples of what you should be doing to improve conversions. Don't assume what they're doing is better, even if they're making more sales than you. Use your own data, your own ideas, and your own test results to make your

decisions. If you are going to borrow ideas, you still need to test them. Make sure you are tracking the Bottom Line Conversion Rate and considering how these ideas affect your business from a holistic perspective.

- *Beware of data coming from qualitative sources like surveys.* Asking people what they *would* do or what they *think* they'd like is relying on theoretical behavior. They might think they'll behave one way but in reality they might do something completely different. You can use this data for ideas, but you should be sure you have confirmed the data with strategies like "Test Before You Test."

- *Don't spend too much money or time on market research data.* Another common mistake I see is people spending too much money on market research data. I've seen companies spend millions of dollars with market research firms, and at the end of the day, they might have some really great data. But they could've easily received better data on real-life behavior if they had put that money into building a simple "Test Before You Test" scenario. This is why hiring the right conversion consultant is critical if you are a high-dollar company. He or she can save you thousands or even millions to get your answers, which brings us to the next mistake . . .

- *Beware of data gathered from friends.* Another data gathering method that I see people use all the time is asking their friends. If you're asking your friends, you're going to be getting some very skewed data. Your friends and associates are probably one of the worst focus groups you could have because they probably don't see things the same way as your prospects or your customers do, and they're often going to tell you what they think you want to hear (or the opposite, depending on their personality). I see companies asking questions like:

  - Does my website look good?
  - Do you think it should be green?
  - Do you think this would be better if the Buy Now button were here?

  In general, the best way to use friends is just the way you would use a focus group. Use them to try to identify things that you may have not thought of already. You don't want help rationalizing your ideas. The test results are what matter. So, always test.

Build Your Skills

The skills lab for this chapter will help you learn more about what data to gather and how to apply it to your own business.

You can find this skills lab at www.ConvertEveryClick.com/chapter5

Hook Me Up, Benji!

Get access to FREE 30-day trial of Crazy Egg.
Get access to FREE ClickTale account.
Go to www.ConvertEveryClick.com/hookmeup

CHAPTER SIX

Conversion-Centric Design

There was a time in my life when I was a full-time web designer, but I never seemed to get along perfectly with other graphic designers. It took some time to understand why, but I eventually figured out that we had fundamental differences in how we looked at design. It turned out that although I was a designer, I was not a graphic artist. Simply put, I did not lead with my artist foot. I was an entrepreneur first. For me, everything I did on a website had to make sense for the user and for the business first. Making it pretty and stylish was important to me, but that was a secondary consideration. This was almost the exact opposite of how most traditional graphic designers viewed their work. Over time through my entrepreneurial endeavors, I realized how important this distinction was.

Once I realized this distinction, I stopped calling myself a designer or graphic artist because it was confusing people (and myself). Traditional design is focused on the ideals of beauty and other elements, such as branding. Although these things are important, they are just one small factor on a website from a conversion rate optimization (CRO) perspective. From my point of view, the business's bottom line is the most important thing, and any element that adds to that is important. Any element that hurts the bottom line, or bottom line potential, needs to be reconsidered and most likely revised, even if it's beautiful. My preference is to get the best of both worlds. I'm a visual person, and I like things to be pretty and cool, too, but not at the cost of lower conversions, unless it's 100 percent intentional. At my web development company, ClickCore, we try to shoot for a website that converts well, while still maintaining the beauty and "coolness."

Design is another example of how I tend to look at things from a customer-centric, holistic conversion perspective, where the customer is at the center of the focus. Let me clarify what I mean by that. The design industry's typical business model is to make their clients happy, not necessarily to make their clients more money. Because their client is the company, their work usually winds up being company-centric, not customer-centric. If the company is happy, the website must be good, and therefore, they did a good job.

I've talked to many designers and tried to explain that their design may be beautiful or even really cool, but that doesn't mean that it will get the conversions it needs. In fact, beauty-based design innovations can often block conversions (while looking really good doing it). I have hired employees from the design world, and I have even hired design agencies myself when I wanted cool branding, so I am not saying they don't have a place. But, I also know their limitations, and it's important that you do, too.

It comes down to understanding this concept. Designers' opinions will often conflict with fundamental conversion concepts because these concepts often prevent them from being extremely creative. One of my favorite examples of this concept relates to the popular newspaper publishing term known as 'above the fold' (which I'll explain soon for those not familiar with the term). Marketing principles have supported the idea that what is above the fold on your website is most important. In some cases, online marketers have polarized this idea by saying that everything should fit above the fold if you want to convert someone.

The design industry likes to set and follow trends. Recent trends in design are trying to fight the idea that what's above the fold matters. Many polarizing design related articles now conclude that people have learned to scroll more, which supports designer's ability to be more creative. But this narrow view is flawed in multiple ways. First, we have significant data from split tests and heat map scroll tracking that proves that what's above the fold is still very important in most cases. Does that mean you have to fit everything at the top of your website to get conversions? Or, does it mean that all websites can be as long as you want because people are starting to scroll more? The answer is neither and both. It depends on the situation, the user context, and the offer. The only way to know for sure on your site and with your audience is to test it yourself.

But, generally speaking, what is above the fold is often the most important part of your page. If you don't do a good job above the fold, a large percentage of visitors will never convert. Either they didn't find what they were looking for above the fold, or they weren't interested enough to scroll down.

That concept creates a frustrating problem for designers. Why? Because often everything doesn't fit above the fold and designers don't usually like clutter. Clean and simple design is a popular style. For this reason, designers can find multiple articles supporting the idea that 'above the fold' doesn't matter anymore.

Again, keep in mind, designers are not doing this maliciously. They are looking for supporting evidence to enable them to be more creative. It's a psychological fact of human nature that people tend to look for evidence proving that they are correct, and they will almost always find it. We've all done this at some point whether we know it or not.

Traditionally, designers have achieved satisfaction by the verbal, written, or facial expressions of approval from their clients or managers. But, if your explicit goal is to increase conversion rates, the success of a design must be measured by the results of the split test.

Don't get me wrong, we need good designers because we like things to be pleasing to the eye. But, it's important to understand where designers are coming from so that you can work with them most effectively. Because the job of a designer is to make things look good, it makes sense that they might have a hard time thinking from a business perspective where profits are often more important than beauty. Since it can be difficult to find a great conversion-centric designer, learning these principles will help you collaborate effectively with your designer.

Universal Conversion Logic

You might have flipped to this chapter hoping to find specific recommendations for graphic design: how many columns you should have, what colors you should use, and other things such as that. There are lots of experts and books out there that will recommend things like "An orange button converts best," or "Larger text will get read first." These ideas are called "best practices," but these kinds of best practices work only *some* of the time. They have tested true for certain businesses, but they might not work for yours. Then where are you? Stuck buying another book hoping to find better best practices.

The only way to know for sure what's the best practice for you is to test it. This is why I prefer to teach what I call Universal Conversion Logic (UCL). That's what you're going to learn in this chapter. I want you to understand the logic *behind* why blue works better than red in some cases or why (and when) a smaller graphic might work better than a larger one. You will get better results when you know *why* and *when* certain ideas work. Once you know how the brain works, including basic psychology and logic, you can start establishing your own best practices unique to your business prospects and customers in a way that best suits your company. Then you'll be able to design higher converting split tests and actually understand what's going on when you see the results.

Where Do You Start?

The first place we look is the overall website design. If you're starting from scratch, great! You can design your website with conversion in mind right from the start. That's what conversion-centric design is all about. We're not talking about conversion as an accessory to the website; we're talking about putting conversion at the center of the website plan. But if you have a huge website with hundreds of pages to change, it's easy to get overwhelmed. If that's you, perhaps you could start by improving one page at a time. Testing something is better than testing nothing.

Remember, although it's true that the entire website works together to affect conversion, each microconversion point is part of that process.

Which page do you start with? When in doubt, start with the place in the funnel where most people have to pass through to get to your bottom line conversion. If most people have to go through your product page to buy your product, then it probably makes sense to start making improvements on the product page.

Don't overwhelm yourself by thinking you have to do everything all at once. You have to start somewhere, so you're better off just picking something and going for it than doing nothing at all. Testing is all about experimentation, so don't try to plan everything out all at once. You can learn along the way. One of the worst things you can do is spend months and months planning a test. Just jump in and run the test.

This is where a conversion rate optimization specialist may be valuable to you because of his or her experience alone. We can help you figure out the best place to start to get the biggest return on your investment. If you don't have a consultant on your side, figure out what you already know and then start testing. Don't try to plan everything out in advance, because you can't know everything before you test. Every website is different, user contexts are different, conversions change from industry to industry—you get the point.

Visitors Evaluate Your Page in a Fraction of a Second

Have you ever heard of the "lizard brain"? It's that part of the human brain that subconsciously evaluates everything around us in microseconds. It decides whether something is important enough for us to pay attention to, if that thing can be trusted, or if we should run away in fear. It senses danger and gives us gut feelings that we may not even realize we're having. Basically, it's our instinct.

The lizard brain plays a large role in your conversion rates, too. There are three Psychological Conversion Checkpoints your brain goes through in a fraction of a second before the conscious mind even sees a web page: Is this page *relevant?* Is it *credible?* Is what they're offering a good enough *value* to get the conversion? (See Figure 6.1.) The value will sometimes be checked by the lizard brain, such as when you subconsciously decide

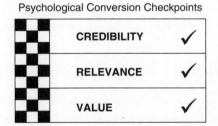

Psychological Conversion Checkpoints

CREDIBILITY	✓
RELEVANCE	✓
VALUE	✓

Figure 6.1 The lizard brain evaluates the first two Psychological Conversion Checkpoints before the conscious brain even registers what it's looking at. The third checkpoint, value, takes a little longer and is handled by your prospect's conscious mind.

whether you can afford to buy the item pictured. But often your offer has to pass the value checkpoint again during the conscious decision-making phase later on.

Let's start with a simple example. You may have heard something about bounce rate, which is the percentage of people who land on a page and then bounce right back to Google (or wherever they came from). A high bounce rate or a low "time on page" in your web analytics tells us something's not quite right with the page. People aren't seeing what they expect to see right away. If you know this is a problem for you, it is likely that your visitors' brains are not making it through the Conversion Checkpoints successfully. So this may indicate where you might need to start when trying to fix the problem. The ultimate goal is to make your prospect's lizard brain happy by providing a web page design that passes these checkpoints with flying colors. If the design doesn't pass, the visitor may still stick around and maybe even convert, but it's a lot easier if the design meets these three criteria right out of the gate.

Take an objective look at the page and ask yourself:

- Is it relevant to the audience?
- Does it have a credible feel to my target visitors? Does it look professional enough to trust?
- Is the offer a good value? Does it come close to visitors' true desire?
- Is the offer clear enough to be understood in the amount of time they are visiting?

If your answer is *no* to any of these questions, there's a good place to start revising your page. But don't just guess or rely on your own gut feelings; gather as much data as you can to help provide the answers.

How Important Is Branding for Conversion?

People in the design industry are always talking about how branding is the most important thing to your business. Your logo, your colors, your name—everything that makes up your brand is front and center in their minds. In the off-line world, where you want people to remember you and eventually buy from you, I would most often agree this is true. But in the context of online conversion, the goal is to get a purchase (or some sort of conversion), which makes the importance of good branding more relative. In most cases, credibility is far more important than having a great brand.

When it comes to conversion, branding is mostly a representative of credibility and occasionally value. But having a recognizable brand is often less important than you'd think. If an unknown brand can pass the three Conversion Checkpoints, that's what matters. Unlike the off-line world, you can even split test branding online with little relative cost to see which converts best. So don't let your branding efforts get in the way of your goals online.

Using Colors and Contrast

Designers and business owners tend to get so focused on the colors in their branding that they don't realize how the placement of colors and the contrast on the page can also affect conversion rates. I realize you may not have much choice if you already have an established brand, but it's still important to use your colors and contrast in your favor.

The truth is there are no consistently right or wrong colors for conversion. But the way that you color your page and the concentration of colors on certain spots on a page can subconsciously affect the users and significantly affect the way that they interact with your page. Although this is already happening on your page, it's important to use this set of logic to improve conversions purposefully. Let's look at a basic example: If you have an entire page that's mostly black and white, and you use one bright red element in the bottom right corner, visitors' eyes are going to be drawn to the bright red element very quickly because it stands out from the rest of the page. While that may seem obvious to you, the same logic is true when the difference is more subtle.

Every color also has a contrast. One definition of contrast is the difference in luminance or color that makes an object distinguishable against another object in the same field of view. In other words, contrast makes one object *stand out* and be more visible when viewed against something, such as a background or another object on the page. To a colorblind person, a blue and a red object with the same contrast may look like the exact same shade of gray. High contrast draws the eyes subconsciously toward an element and makes it stand out. Low contrast makes elements blend and not stand out.

An example I love to use to explain contrast is the old TV show *I Love Lucy*. On the show, they always talked about Lucy's bright red hair. But in the early days of the show, viewers couldn't really tell because it was shown in black and white. Viewers had to use their imagination because the only thing you could see was the contrast of the colors, but not the color itself. She could have dyed her hair green as a prank, and it would not have stopped them from taping. Once Lucille Ball started working on shows filmed in color, you could see her red hair and it stood out.

One type of contrast is how bright or dark a certain color is on a spectrum of black to white, like in the Lucy example, but there's also a contrast type that is a relative value referring to the contrast of two or more colors in relation to each other. If you want something to stand out, you want high contrast—colors that are very different from each other. If you want something to be less of a priority for your visitor, perhaps you might consider testing lowering its relative contrast.

For example, a black background with small white text is often hard to read because the contrast is so high. The background stands out and you have to squint to read the text. But if you flip it and have a white background with black text, suddenly it's easy to read because the color is standing out rather than the background. That's one reason why books are printed with black ink on white paper.

You can use these concepts to help guide people's eyes to where you want them to go. If everything else on the page is the same, the eye will likely be drawn to the biggest contrast ratio of dark to light (Figure 6.2).

A few years ago there was a graphic design fad where designers would put text on websites in gray instead of black because it was thought to be prettier and easier on the eye. Unfortunately, if you need people to actually read your text, that low contrast could hurt your conversion rates because it's harder to read. The eye may even glaze over it. In contrast—pun intended—you can use that idea to do the opposite. If you have parts of the page you must have there for SEO compliance, or prospects who like to research, but you don't care if people read it, then it might be smart to test turning down the contrast some. Maybe have 80 percent contrast instead of 100 percent contrast in the areas you want people to skim over. Keep your headline and important elements at 100 percent contrast.

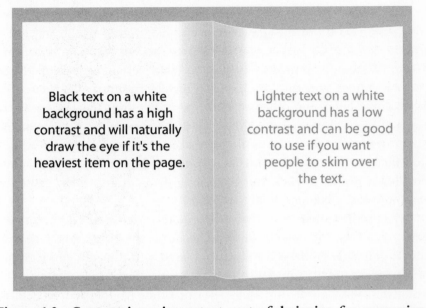

Black text on a white background has a high contrast and will naturally draw the eye if it's the heaviest item on the page.

Lighter text on a white background has a low contrast and can be good to use if you want people to skim over the text.

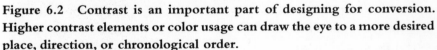

Figure 6.2   Contrast is an important part of designing for conversion. Higher contrast elements or color usage can draw the eye to a more desired place, direction, or chronological order.

When people look at your web page, their eyes are going to consciously be weighted in certain places. This is what I call the visual weight of the element. It's all about the weight of the elements you want to focus on. Brighter or darker colors will actually weigh that element down, and the visitor's eye almost magnetically rolls to that spot. The same goes for high-contrast or darker elements.

Most websites I've seen over the years often have relatively equal weight on all the elements. There's no single focal point to look at. Or there are too many focal points. Sites that seem confusing or busy have high contrast everywhere. The designer may want everything to be beautifully in focus and doesn't realize the negative effect that may have. It's like walking through Times Square at night with 1,000 lighted signs blinking at you all at once. Where do you focus? It's hard to decide which voice to listen to when everyone is screaming. If you are thinking that your site isn't like that, remember these are exaggerated examples. Subtle differences in contrast or color can change the way a user interacts with your site.

In addition to contrast, colors have certain associations in the brain. You may have heard that green is serene like a grassy field, and red is intense like fire. Or maybe you think green means "go" and red means "stop." We're conditioned from birth to make certain associations based on our culture, and this conditioning usually trumps color rules. Stop signs, traffic lights, and other everyday items reinforce this notion. These types of associations can affect the way that someone reacts to colors on your page. A bright red box might make someone stop and read and lead them to then make a purchase. A green submit button might subtly encourage people to click. But the wrong shade of green may cause the button to lose credibility if it's too bright.

Don't forget that colors have different associations in different cultures, too. Take the color yellow, for example. In North America, yellow is generally a cheerful color, associated with the sun and summer and happiness. In Latin America and Egypt, however, yellow can be associated with mourning and loss. But other Middle Eastern countries often treat yellow more like North America, as a happy color. Just be aware of your audience and what colors might mean to them.

So look at your page and decide where the focal elements should be. Then either punch the contrast up on those elements, or tone down other elements on the page. Examine contrast not just for the page but also for elements within elements, including the text on a button. Use this concept to help your visitor's eye prioritize elements on your page. Keep in mind color and contrast are two different things. Although all colors have contrast, some colors shine brighter on the screen. Use these Universal Conversion Logic principles to your advantage, and don't forget to test your results.

Using the Eye–Blur Technique to Evaluate Element Weights

We've already talked about eye tracking and mouse tracking—special hardware and software that tracks a visitor's eyes and mouse movement, where they go, and how they interact with the page. But the technology and processes required for eye tracking can be very expensive, and you usually need a completed page to use.

When you're trying to make design decisions, especially if you're a small-business owner or your budget is limited, we like to recommend using what we call the Eye–Blur Technique. The idea is to literally look at the screen and squint your eyes until your vision is unfocused and the screen is blurry (or if you wear glasses like I do, just take them off).

Certain things are going to happen when you do this. Small text on the page should fade away, and lower contrast elements, such as gray text on a white background, will fade away so much that you probably won't even see them. Other brighter or high-contrast elements or colors will stand out. You'll instantly see how the page is weighted for the user based on the colors and contrasts.

If you can still read your headline when the rest of the page is pretty much blurred out, it's a good sign that the user will read that headline first. If you can't read it, you might even consider increasing the font size or color contrast. If you have that bright red element in the corner and everything else is black and white, when you blur your eyes, you're going to see a big gray area and then a red block in the corner. You won't be able to stop your eye from being drawn to that red block (see Figure 6.3).

This is a good way to get a glimpse at what your prospect's initial subconscious lizard brain may see when first looking at your page. The lizard brain also calculates what to look at, and in what priority order, in that fraction of a second before the conscious brain catches up. These decisions are not as voluntary as people think. If you do a good job of calling attention to the correct focus points, you'll be well on your way to higher conversion rates.

Figure 6.3 Use the Eye–Blur Technique to quickly evaluate how elements such as size, color, and contrast affect how portions of your page are weighted.

How Page Layout Affects Conversions

Layout is one of the most important design concepts to comprehend when it comes to affecting conversion rates. Perhaps you've noticed newspaper layouts have hardly changed at all in more than a century. Yes, this is partly because people are familiar with the layout, and people don't like change. However, it's mostly because the format works really well. Publishers have optimized it to the point where it's pretty much a perfect system. It's highly measureable, and there are over 100 years of data to support it.

The front page contains the main headline and feature picture to capture your attention and draw you in. Traditionally, "draw you in" literally meant it enticed you to open the sales box or stop at the stand and buy the paper. The headline was also what the paperboy would yell out on the street corner to get you to buy the paper. The side panels are reserved for secondary articles, advertising, and some smaller catchy articles to engage you further. Magazine covers use a similar concept but with a different layout. The picture draws you in, and the headlines make you want to open and read. They have the high-quality color advantages, too; newspapers are larger, but the color is dull or even just black and white. The whole format is designed to capture your attention and entice you into opening it and hopefully purchasing it.

Even though people seem to think every website layout needs to be reinvented from scratch, in reality, the same Universal Conversion Logic principles still apply. You probably still want to use larger text and pictures to draw attention to the focal point. And you still need well-written headlines and content to engage the audience.

As we mentioned in the introduction on Universal Conversion Logic, people typically analyze and interpret a page based on how they read it in their native language. For example, people accustomed to reading in English typically analyze from left to right and top to bottom. On the other hand, Hebrew or Arabic readers start from the right. We elaborate on this with examples in this chapter's online Skills Lab. For now, just keep this principle in mind when designing your layout. We know from newspaper layout design that what's above the fold has to entice a purchase. But have you heard of the term "above the fold" in relation to CRO (see Figure 6.4)?

Figure 6.4 It's important to understand how your visitors' fold lines affect their interaction with your web page. Knowing the fold line's location for different users is important.

Although a website is not the same as a newspaper, similar logic applies on a basic level. The area above the fold on a website is everything you can see before you start to scroll down. The first screen people see influences whether they're going to continue on that website or go someplace else.

What's above the fold still matters—just like it's mattered on newspapers for more than a century. I doubt the concept will ever go away completely (until websites are 3-D, but we'll save that lesson for another time).

The debates regarding "long vs. short" and "above-the-fold" are interlaced with many Universal Conversion Logic principles throughout this book. Later in the chapter on landing pages, we discuss the debate on when it's appropriate to design a long landing page that requires scrolling versus a simpler above-the-fold landing page. Similarly, in the copywriting chapter, we discuss when to write in longer story format compared to bullet format. In short, it all comes down to your product, offer, and the user context.

On landing pages especially, improving the area above the fold almost always accounts for increases in conversion rates. The time spent below the fold is significantly lower. One of the more common exceptions to this rule that I've seen is on blogs or online resources, such as the *Huffington Post*, where the goal is engagement and keeping people on the website longer, not buying something quickly. In this case, time spent below the fold is more important because the goal is to get people to engage more and come back, as opposed to buying a product. But even on the *Huffington Post*, having a good headline is important to get people to read below the fold, and they are known for using newspaper-like headlines for this reason. In this case, the conversion rate is based on page views or clicks, and getting people below the fold is important. However, if the content above the fold stinks, they're not going to get people to keep reading lower. So the above-the-fold concept still stands.

Using Eyelines to Create Clarity, Direction, and Focus

The use of eyelines is another traditional layout concept that translates from off-line to online media. Eyelines are the lines that show you separations vertically and horizontally. They help you identify certain sections and areas of the page. Whether they are physical lines or white space, eyelines create clear separations between different sections of your page so it looks clean, not jumbled or busy.

Vertical columns and horizontal rows are good examples of natural eyelines. Think of eyelines as guides for your visitor. You can use clearly defined eyelines to help the reader's eye know where to look on the page (see Figure 6.5). For example, websites such as Pinterest use vertical eyelines to encourage people to keep scrolling.

Elements such as arrows and photos can also be used to create eyelines. For example, if a person in a photo on your page appears to be looking directly at your call-to-action, chances are good that your site visitor will subconsciously follow that line of sight to its end point. We will dive deeper into creative layout principles like these in the Skills Lab for this chapter.

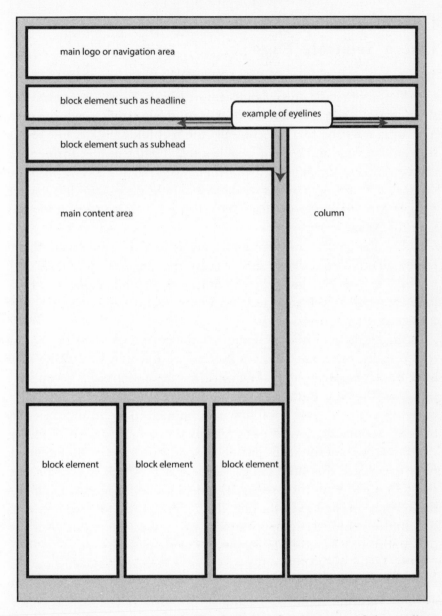

Figure 6.5 **The arrows in this illustration point to some of the eyelines on this layout.**

Consider Treating Each Foldpage Like a Separate Page

We talked earlier about "above the fold" being the area you see on a web page before you scroll down. Foldpages are essentially the screen areas that show within a single screen window as someone scrolls down the page. The area above the fold is technically the first foldpage. Because screen sizes are different, and because people scroll at different speeds, foldpages can be different for different people. They are not as easily definable as pages in a book would be. As we discussed in the data-gathering chapter, Google Analytics and tools like Crazy Egg can help you better identify your foldpages.

Now that you know what a foldpage is, and you understand that it can be different on different devices, you may consider optimizing each foldpage to your best advantage. In other words, think about each fold-page as a separate web page, and then figure out how you might improve it to get higher conversion rates.

One example of how to optimize a foldpage might be adding a call to action for each one. This can increase conversions by making your offer once per screen, instead of once for the entire page. If you have only one Buy Now button, and it's all the way at the bottom of the page, many people will never scroll down far enough to see it, and they may be ready sooner. Of course, you probably don't want to have 17 identical Buy Now buttons; that's just obnoxious. But you can find different ways to achieve the same thing. Maybe add a "check it out" link on one foldpage, a button on the next, and a product image with a link in the caption on the next. Not only does adding a call to action on each screen give people more opportunities to convert, but it also gives you the opportunity to target different types of people.

On traditional sales websites, people who scroll down below the first fold tend to be the people who are research minded and want to learn every detail about your product, so opt-in offers, such as educational guides, lengthy tutorials, and demos tend to work better below the fold. Spontaneous or quick-decision personalities will act on their impulses above the fold, so a call to action in the form of a button, link, or short capture web form would be good to put above the fold. Consider matching your call to action to the personality type most likely to convert in each location (above or below the fold). And don't forget you'll have all types of personalities coming to your website, so consider accommodating them all in different ways.

I like to think of this as helping your visitor exit through the gift shop, so to speak. You know how museums and theme parks often place the exit on the other side of the gift shop, forcing you to walk through the shop to leave? It's a brilliant plan, and it probably accounts for a healthy percentage of their revenue. You can do the same thing with your foldpages. Provide a way for visitors to exit each foldpage and make the exit go through the gift shop.

What does that mean, exactly? Well, one example is having a call to action, as we just noted. Another example is having the shopping cart follow visitors as they scroll down the page of an e-commerce website. Another example is including more subtle links within the content that navigate to product description pages. The idea is if you're going to let the visitors navigate away from the current page, take them someplace that gets them closer to a conversion.

Responsive Design

What happens to your beautiful, expensive website when someone views it on a mobile phone or iPad? Until recently, people didn't think about how the design would appear on different devices because the mobile technology was relatively new. They only thought about their own computer and how it looked there. But eyelines, foldpages, content, and images became a big jumble, depending on the tablet or phone you were viewing on. Every phone had a different screen size, and more devices seemed to hit the market every day. Devices such as tablets and mobile phones snuck up on designers and eventually made the industry start thinking about how screen sizes affect the user's experience. Slowly, more people are starting to realize that a user's experience with their website is different from the experience with these other devices.

Responsive design is making this evolution easier, thank goodness. Unfortunately, it can make conversion optimization and split testing more complicated. A responsive website figures out what device a viewer is using and rearranges the design accordingly. This all happens automatically and predictably if you designed the website that way. Designers are now creating websites in different sizes and letting the responsive technology automatically show the correct design for the different devices. It can even create a unique design fitted to the individual's screen based on some settings created by the designer.

Responsive design gives you the ability to change the layout dynamically based on the size of the screen (Figure 6.6). You maintain control over where the eyelines are and what's above the fold. This control can be extremely important in terms of conversion rates—whether your goal is moving them to another page, buying a product on a landing page, or signing up for a free download.

Companies that have mastered responsive design and conversion strategies behind it are really standing out above the rest in conversion metrics. It's often important to make sure you hire a design firm that can deliver a responsive site. But don't take my word for it. Do some data gathering using Google Analytics to see the different devices and screen sizes your visitors are using. Is there enough traffic to make improving conversions on mobile worth evaluating? Only your data can answer that, but also consider national data gathering from market research firms for this. You'll

Figure 6.6 Responsive design is a technology that changes the layout and structure of your page based on the individual user's screen size and/ or device. Remember, the more customer-centric you can get, the easier it is to optimize for the individual.

be able to make a more informed decision after seeing the trends toward mobile in your industry. For the next while, it might be difficult to find a design firm that understands conversion rate optimization on top of that, so choose your designers wisely.

It's extremely complicated to track conversions through split-testing strategies on responsive sites. Tracking is getting easier, though, which is great because it's getting more and more important to split test for different devices as millions of people switch to consuming web content on mobile devices. Later in the book, we will discuss mobile site design and go a bit deeper into this topic.

Common Mistakes to Avoid with Graphic Design

- *Don't forget nonvisual elements.* Persuasive text is just as important as a pleasing visual design. Sometimes it's even more important. If you're selling something high priced or something that needs a lot of explanation, the text can be critical to conversion. I've seen people waste hundreds of thousands of dollars on ideas that were visually focused when they could increase conversions significantly by focusing on other things, such as the message or written offer.

- *Don't forget your text is part of your design, too.* The way your text looks on the page is an important part of the overall graphic design. Fonts should be easy to read. Don't opt for pretty over easy to read, unless it's been tested and you implement it on purpose. Italics are another "beware" online because they can be hard to read. If you need to emphasize a word or phrase, use underlining, bolding, or color and contrast.

  People are rapidly losing tolerance for hype, so the old landing page styles with the huge red headlines, underlining, bold, and loads of exclamation points just don't convert as well as they used to. They can sometimes make the website look less credible. If used skillfully, these elements are okay, but be careful not to overhype your page. Again, though, that doesn't mean it won't convert for you. Test it, if you want, and see if it provides you with the desired results.

- *Don't use responsive design if it's unnecessary.* From a trend perspective, using responsive design makes sense. From a microconversion perspective, it might make sense, too. But if you're thinking in terms of *holistic* conversion, it's important to look at your entire market and industry before embarking on such a big endeavor to see if it's even worth it for your bottom line.

I see many companies investing a lot of money in responsive design when it's really unnecessary. Although it's true people are moving to smaller and smaller screens, you have to judge your product and your audience to see if it really makes sense for you. It can take a lot of energy, time, and money to make three or more different versions of your website. Split testing can be complicated and time-consuming as well. You have to judge your audience and how fast they're adopting mobile technology. Look at your analytics, learn who your audience is, and find out what devices they're using. Take a look at the statistics over time to make more informed decisions and prioritize your online design improvements and tasks.

- *Don't be too flashy*. Remember when everyone had to have a Flash-animated introduction page on their website or they weren't cool? This is what I've always called "Flash Syndrome": people spend so much time making things "cool" that they ignore conversions. Really cool, unique interactive environments might make you stand out and might win you a design award, but in most cases they actually hurt conversion rates because people don't know how to interact with your website. A good balanced use of animation is a better approach. We will discuss this a bit later in the advanced strategies chapter.

  For example, I've had multiple customers over the years who have said something like this: "I'd love to have a shopping cart on my website that's more like a shopping cart at the grocery store. I want them to actually drag the product into the shopping cart and they can see it shrinking or floating into the shopping cart or something really cool and animated like that."

  I've had to explain to them why most people who had that idea years ago eventually abandoned it. People are used to interacting with a website in a certain way. Online, people are used to the *Add to Cart* or *Buy Now* buttons. Although an animation like that is cool and seems like it would be easier, people often aren't yet ready for that when it comes to maintaining or improving conversions. In cases where websites have implemented something like this, conversions are less than they could be because the visitors don't know how to actually buy. They're thinking, "Where's the Add to Cart button? Why isn't anything happening?" Anytime you violate a universal expectation, you will often see poor results. It's hard to change universal expectations. So when it comes to the bottom line, it's rarely worth trying. The key thing here is that "cool" is great if you're trying to impress your friends or go viral, but cool may not be great if you're trying to create a high-converting website.

- *Don't use Web Fail.0.* Sometimes you can have too much of a good thing. Take Web 2.0 design, for example. Yes, certain elements, such as rounded corners, diagonal lines, and 3-D effects, can be great, but a few years ago, I wrote an article about how people were overdoing it. Whenever we see a website that is obviously overdoing Web 2.0 design, we call it Web Fail.0, because that's what badly done Web 2.0 elements do in testing—they fail to convert. Why? It's mainly because they're trying too hard. It just doesn't look right to the eye, and it also hurts credibility.

  You may know a Web Fail.0 site when you see one. It looks like a cartoon with exaggerated images, rounded corners, gradients, and 3-D text. It looks amateurish and doesn't come across as genuine or professional to the reader. You lose credibility, so naturally, conversion suffers.

  Now, don't get me wrong. Web 2.0 designs can be done well. However, it takes a gifted designer to pull it off. The key is subtle application of Web 2.0 elements so that you don't notice the design, only the content. But subtle seems so hard to do online for many designers, so we tend to recommend that people just stay away from these elements unless their designer is very, very good.

  Designers who are good at Web 2.0 have since evolved their design skills to what I call Web 3.0, which is using the beauty and simplicity of 2.0 in ways that are more functional, credible, and better for conversion.

- *Don't forget to take everything a designer or agency says with a grain of salt.* As I've mentioned over and over again in this chapter, designers and design agencies will often try to give you what you want, which may not be what you need. Take everything they say with a grain of salt, and let the test results be the final authority on what designs you stick with.

Build Your Skills

The skills lab for this chapter will dive deeper into the topics of layout alignment and eyelines. It will also help you recognize where a page is weighted and how to change where the weight appears.

You can find this skills lab at www.ConvertEveryClick.com/chapter6

CHAPTER SEVEN

Conversion-Centric Copywriting

First, let's define the word *copy*. Copy is all the text that makes up your headlines, offers, value proposition, product descriptions, pay-per-click (PPC) ads, and e-mails—any writing involved in your marketing and sales. When people used to ask me to explain conversion rate optimization (CRO) to them, often I'd broadly explain that roughly half of CRO is about tweaking and testing design and layout on a web page, and half is about the message and words on the page. That's not to be taken literally, but it does do a good job of explaining the importance of copy when it comes to CRO.

With HCRO, I now talk about the three elements of the Psychological Conversion Checklist: relevance, credibility, and value. In most cases, it's difficult to pass all three checkpoints with graphics alone; you need copy. It works the other way, too. Sales letters on a white background without visuals are usually not enough. If you look at a website in a language you don't understand, you will know how difficult it is for you to evaluate the website without copy that represents relevance, credibility, and has enough value to convert into a sale. Even if the website has a great visual design, you'll probably miss something without the words.

While there's a time and place where more copy converts better, generally speaking, there's less tolerance for words. So well-written, persuasive copy can affect the page significantly. What you say in the space allotted is exponentially more important. For example, I've changed an eight-word headline and increased conversions on the entire page by more than 366 percent, just by lifting the relevance and value of the words cho-sen. Although this particular example is an above-average improvement, it shows how important the right words can be in CRO.

There can be an ongoing argument in business and copywriting circles about whether long copy or short copy is better. It all depends on the user context of the individual reading it. Split testing is the only way to know for sure how much copy you need to use for your product and your audience. There is some Universal Conversion Logic you can use, though, that says the more commonly understood and less expensive a product is, the less copy you need. We will go more in depth on this topic in the chapter on landing pages.

In the previous chapter we talked about how design plays a role in the Conversion Checkpoints. However, the design by itself is only half of the story. Alone it means nothing. Conversely, to an extremely visual person, copy means nothing without design. Generally speaking, your website is incomplete unless both factors are considered—the design and the copy. While the general rule I use to explain the copy-to-visuals ratio is 50/50, it changes depending on the individual visitor's learning style. People who learn or communicate best through the written word will convert better through the copy portion of the page.

Copy contributes to the value side of the checklist by conveying the offer or the message in persuasive terms. People need to know what they're getting and how it's valuable to them. Copy can contribute to credibility by talking about guarantees, achievements such as awards or media appearances, or by giving testimonials and endorsements. The style of the writing and words used in sales copy can make a product sound more credible or less credible depending on the user context. Copy can contribute to relevance (and value) with things like headlines, subheads, body copy, and all other text elements related to an offer.

Copywriting for conversion is a skill well worth developing. If you don't like to write, hiring a skilled conversion copywriter is a really good idea. Even with all the time and money we spend optimizing visual design for conversion, if the words on the page aren't persuasive or rel-evant, you may not get the conversions you're hoping for. Some of the easiest increases in conversion come from changing the copy because of the importance of its role in all three Conversion Checkpoints.

I don't like to claim I'm a copywriter, formally, but I am a conversion rate optimizer. I understand how copy influences conversion. I have mul-tiple copywriters on staff specifically to assist in the brainstorming process and take new copy ideas and concepts to the next level. The foundational knowledge is what's important.

In this chapter, we're going to talk about the Universal Conversion Logic (UCL) of copywriting, as we did in the design chapter. It's important to understand *why* a headline or piece of body copy works so that you can recognize what changes might bring about an increase in your conversion rate. Many of these ideas and strategies are rooted in psychological principles. Studying psychology and human behavior can be a great benefit to your business.

Customer-Centric Copy

It's a known psychological principle that human beings are, at the most basic level, inherently concerned about themselves when making decisions. (Yes, even me and you, no matter how selfless we think we are.) It's a survival tactic that goes back to the beginning of time. So when most people visit a website, whether they realize it or not, their lizard brains are thinking, "What's in it for me?" In other words, what can a business, service, or product do for me? Can it solve my problem or make my life better in some way?

On the other hand, the owner of the website is also thinking about himself or herself. Very often, the copy on the website is very company-centric, saying things such as, "We have the best widgets anywhere," or "Come check out our great deals." In this case, the website owner is trying to provide credibility and value, which is great, but the visitor is also looking for relevance and value from their perspective. That's why we covered the concept of the Ideal Conversion Point in Chapter 3, to help you see how you can find the sweet-spot where your needs overlap the visitors needs to create a conversion.

Business websites tend to have company-centric slogans, such as: "*I* offer accounting services for veterans," "*We* sell pet toys," or "*We* have the best roofers around."

Do you see how those phrases are company-centric? If they say *I* or *we*, it's usually a dead giveaway that the copy probably revolves around the business and what it does. This is common, but UCL says, you should think about it from the visitor's perspective. It's important to test the copy with *customer-centric* language. What are they going to get? Although I'm exaggerating a little to make it clear, those same phrases could be rewritten like this:

- As a veteran, *you* can access discount accounting services here.
- *Your* pets deserve toys this awesome!
- Get *your* roof repaired by an expert *you* can trust.

See the difference? Basically, all I did was turn the words *I* and *we* into *you* and *your*. Just shifting the perspective of your writing can make a huge difference to your conversions. People immediately get the message that you're concerned about them and their problem or need. With company-centric writing, your prospect has to translate it to what that means for them, which can serve as another step preventing them from converting.

These are some basic examples so that you get the idea. We didn't talk about the context in these examples, and there's still more to learn. So don't take these sentences literally and run with them. I want to be very clear that these are conceptual examples.

How to Use The Get Principle to Write More Customer-Centric Copy

In Chapter 3, we talked about using The Get principle for opt-in web forms, but it works in other places, too, including slogans and headlines. The foundation of The Get principle is using active, customer-centric language. It tells the customers what they're going to get.

If people reading a page are asking, "What's in it for me?" then your best bet to increase conversions is to give them what they want. People want to get something:

- They want to get information.
- They want to get a product or service.
- They want to get self-esteem.
- They want to get confirmation that they were right about something.

Whatever they want in your example, give it to them. But don't tell them what you're going to give them, tell them what they're going to get. That's the real difference between company- and customer-centric copy. It's *give* versus *get*. You want to write in terms of *getting*, even though you're doing the giving.

For example, say you sell tennis shoes. Why do people come to your website? To get tennis shoes. So, when you write a call to action in a link or a button, a good place to start your thought process is to say something like, "Get tennis shoes," or "Get your tennis shoes now." You're forcing yourself to think in the customer-centric perspective. Now, that may not be the best copy in the world, but it's a start. When in doubt, use the word *get* to focus your brain thinking in the right direction.

Using the word *get* in your buttons and links will almost always increase conversions over words such as *submit* or *find out more*. People don't want to submit; *they want to get, so remind them of their side of the exchange, not yours*. You don't have to use this strategy with everything you write, but it really does help start your thinking process in the customer-centric direction for better conversions.

Whenever you're stuck for a headline, you can also use the word *get*, and the sentences will practically write themselves. Here are a couple of basic examples you could test:

Instead of: Red bicycles for sale.

Try: Get your red bicycle today.

Instead of: We guarantee next-day delivery.

Try: Get next-day delivery, guaranteed.

How to Make Your Copy Hyperrelevant

People often struggle with writing sales copy. They feel as though in the deepest point in their heart that they must be eloquent or use elaborate verbiage extrapolated from their cornucopia of internal diction (yes, that means fancy words they know) to convey their intentions. Sometimes fancy words are appropriate for your target audience. For example, if you're selling diamonds or luxury apartments, people expect a certain kind of language. Write to meet your audience's expectations, but, in general, simpler language is often more relatable, and therefore relevant.

The easiest way to make your copy hyperrelevant is to convey your message in their language. One way you could potentially do this is to interview prospects and ask them what they wanted, what they feared, and what they weren't sure of. You would write down everything they said verbatim and then repeat it all back in the sales copy. It was about using *their own words* to sell to them.

The more modern strategy is to research online keywords, forums, question-and-answer websites, and social media groups to see how people are talking about your product or industry. Or you can also use other data gathering methods to discover more about your user's context and the words that might provide the desired result. Are there certain questions that come up over and over again? That might be a good topic to bring up in your copy. Do people talk about your competitors? How can you use that to your advantage?

Another common way to research for copywriting is to find out what keywords people are typing into Google to get to your website. For example, say you're an accountant. What words are people typing into Google to find your website? (Remember, this information is available in your Google Analytics account or in Google's keyword planner.) If lots of people are typing in "how to save for retirement" or "saving for college," you can use those phrases more often in your copy to better sell your services. Using target prospects' exact words is a strategy copywriters have used for decades because it works. As always, don't just take this at face value, test it.

Increasing Relevance and Credibility of Links

As we know, relevance is one of the Conversion Checkpoints (Figure 7.1). The lizard brain can evaluate the relevance of a web page in a fraction of a second. It's looking for immediate clues that it's in the right place, and then the conscious brain takes some time to evaluate the page. So you want to show relevance very clearly. With copy, a good headline and on-page copy is often vital, but another important way to demonstrate relevance is to make sure your links match their destination.

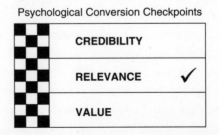

Figure 7.1   Consider the Conversion Checkpoints when making links or clickable ads.

When people see a link in an ad, an e-mail, or a social media post, they have certain expectations. You're promising something if they click that link. Make sure you give them what they're expecting—or you could lose them. You want to make sure your message is clear through each microconversion.

If a PPC ad says, "Get a red truck," and it leads to a page with a picture of a green car, that's not a good match. It doesn't seem like a big deal, but it is. That business spent money for the click, and that money may be completely wasted if it's attracting the wrong people. A bad link-page match can also damage trust built up with the other conversion rate optimization efforts on the page (see Figure 7.2). Not to mention, systems like Google AdWords often reward more linear funnels with better ad rates.

One way to tell if you have a link-page mismatch is to look at your bounce rate in Google Analytics. If a lot of people are clicking through to your page and then bouncing back to Google within a few seconds, that tells you the visitor's lizard brain probably isn't finding what it expected to find. You might think people will surf around the website and figure out where to find what they're looking for, but most of the time they won't bother.

Look at what your links and ads are really saying. What are they promising? Then click the link and see what you're delivering. What probably made perfect sense in your mind when you created the page might be completely off base compared to the link you just came through.

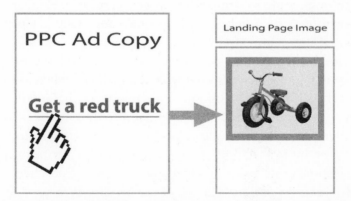

Figure 7.2 This illustration is an example of a mismatch for relevance. The image on the landing page is green (and not a truck). It should be a red truck. Keep your messaging through the funnel as linear as possible. With copy, relevance is still one of the Psychological Conversion Checkpoints.

You may be thinking to yourself, "Why wouldn't we just use the exact same term in the headline and the link?" That's not a bad idea and it might be worth testing. The same logic may be worth testing for matching search keywords to ad and headline. In fact, we've implemented a piece of software we built for our clients that does this dynamically through code. It doesn't work for every situation, but it can definitely help out when you have large volumes of keywords and ad copy. If nothing else, it could be a good place to start testing to get more linear.

Similar to designers, many writers are more in love with words and the beautiful rhythm of language than your results. They can get offended when you want to simplify the message or copy exactly what your prospects are telling you. As with designers, my favorite copywriters are more concerned with my return on investment (ROI) than with their own words. In my experience, it's easier to find copywriters with this quality than designers because writers typically learn the concept of using different writing styles for different audiences early on.

Eight Keys to Writing an Enticing Offer

It doesn't matter how beautiful your site design is, how much traffic you get, or how much data you collect—if you have a crummy offer, you're not going to get the conversions. Now, I'm sure you have a top-notch product or service, at least I hope so, but if you don't write about it correctly, it's not going to come across as being valuable. Here are some tips to help you write a better offer, and how they help get past your prospect's conversion checkpoints.

1. *Base your offer on prospects' true desire.* Remember when we talked about the Ideal Conversion Point? It's that place that intersects the prospects' true desire and your true desire. Make sure your offer is *written* in terms of their desire. The closer you get to what they truly desire, the more they'll be willing to give you in terms of money, information, time, and so on. Relevance: check! Value: check!
2. *Write a persuasive headline.* The job of the headline is to hook the person's attention and keep him or her on the page long enough to make the offer. It should contain some mention of the problem the visitor is trying to solve and/or your solution. Remember The Get principle when writing your headlines. Relevance: check! Value: check!

3. *Prove it!* Prove what? Everything. Just prove everything. In the old days, you may have been able to rely exclusively on hype to sell your product: big, bold red headlines; words in all caps and loads of exclamation points; and so-called magic words such as *skyrocket* and *cash infusion!*

   Just because it's on the Internet doesn't make it true anymore. People like proof. Every claim you make could benefit from some sort of proof behind it, whether that's graphs, screenshots, reputable people or sources, a case study, or testimonials. Anonymous visitors aren't going to take your word that you have the friendliest carpet cleaners in town; prove it if you can—perhaps with testimonials or friendly videos. Credibility: check! Value: check!

4. *List benefits, not just features.* You might have heard this concept before; it goes back to giving versus getting. Features are what you're giving, and benefits are what they are getting.

   Feature: All-metal parts. (That's what you're giving—metal parts.)
   Benefit: Lasts longer due to all-metal parts. (That's what they're getting—more durability.)

   Feature: 24/7 phone support. (Giving support.)
   Benefit: Get help anytime! Phone support standing by for you 24/7.
   (Getting support.)

   Bullet points are a great way to convey benefits quickly, and they help break up the text visually, too, making the copy easier to read. Consider testing alternatives to bullet points, too. Checkmarks and plus signs can sometimes be a better, more positive "get" approach. Value: check! Relevance: check!

5. *Include several calls to action (use buttons, links, and images).* Put at least one call to action above the fold. Then sprinkle a few more throughout the rest of the copy. Vary the way you do this so that you don't come across as pushy. Try a link here, a button there, maybe a link attached to a photograph someplace else. Turn a word in your copy into a link. For example, if you have the sentence "There are many things you can do with our product," make "our product" a link to the product page. There are lots of ways to add subtle calls to action. As we discussed in the graphic design chapter, this is another way to help people "exit through the gift shop" on every foldpage. You're helping them exit *where you want them to go.*

Remember The Get principle when writing your calls to action. People want to get something, so give them what they want and tell them what they will get.

6. *Give bonuses.* People love getting stuff for free. You know those famous commercials on TV? "But wait, there's more! Order one [insert product here], and get two more absolutely *free!*" Did you ever wonder why they didn't just sell a set of three to start with? Because the price for one product sets the expectation, and therefore getting two products for free raises the perceived value of the offer. People feel like they're getting a great deal.

   If they are paying attention long enough to get to that part, they already want to make the purchase. They're just looking for a rational reason why they should go ahead and buy. When you add the value of two free knives, it turns into a no-brainer. People buy on emotion and justify with logic. If people watch a commercial and think, *That's really cool*, they're already 80 percent of the way to the purchase. They just need a rational reason to make the purchase. Added perceived value gives them that rational reason. The TV commercial example is just one way. What can you offer as a bonus item to raise the perceived value?

7. *Make it easy.* Whether they admit it or not, people like things to be easy. Test making your words easier and more positive. Test alternatives to words in your offer that imply visitors have to do something difficult, even if the implication is subtle. Consider using synonyms that don't imply as much work for the visitor. Test alternatives to words that have negative connotations or that make them feel like they're going to lose something to get something.

   Instead of *learn*, you could test *discover*.

   Instead of *build*, you could test *create*.

   Instead of *pay*, you could test *invest*.

8. *Use numbers.* Numbers make things tangible, and they can be a big help in your copy. Test numbers in your headlines, offers, PPC ads, e-mail subject lines—lots of places. They naturally create curiosity and help break up long sections of text by drawing the eye. Here are some examples.

   7 Ways to . . .

   15 Reasons You Should Never . . .

   3 Ideas That Will . . .

Common Mistakes to Avoid with Copywriting

- *Don't assume you're the best person to write your copy.* Even if you're a great writer and you enjoy the process, is it really the best use of your time? If you're fast and come up with great ideas, then maybe it is a good use of time. But having a good writer on your team can really cut down on the time and expense it takes to complete a project. Often people are too close and know too much about their products or services to write their own copy effectively.
- *Don't hire the wrong kind of writer.* All writers write words but not necessarily the kind of words you need. If they call themselves writers, they're probably more concerned with the words and the artistic quality of the writing. If they call themselves copywriters, that's a sign that there is a chance they may be concerned with your ROI. It can be challenging to find a great copywriter, one who is focused on getting results rather than protecting their prose. But no matter who does your writing, as long as you're consistently split testing, you should be able to improve your results.
- *Don't forget to split test your copy.* There are hundreds of ways to say the same thing, especially with sales copy. Just because you come up with a headline you think is awesome (or follows all the "rules" you learned) doesn't mean you shouldn't split test it. Even the top copywriters in the world admit that sometimes they can't tell the winners from the losers in a test. The whole point is things can almost always get better, so once you have a winner, go back to the drawing board and test another option if it's a priority for your HCRO goals.
- *Don't assume all copywriting principles apply.* Context is everything with copy. Not every tool in a copywriter's arsenal should be applied equally in every situation. For example, PPC ads require different techniques than product descriptions. Long-cycle products take a different approach than items with a short sales cycle. Make sure you understand the context of the technique before applying it to your business.
- *Don't use The Get principle everywhere.* The Get principle has its exceptions. Remember, it's intended to be a good starting point. But sometimes you may need to take a *give* approach. For example, in the nonprofit world, people want the satisfaction of giving; that's where the emotional benefit is found. The visitor needs to feel good about

giving something to someone else. In other words, explain what the beneficiary will be getting in return for the gift or donation. It's still technically a *get*, but they are getting to give.

- *Don't use copywriting techniques in educational e-mail, social media, personal stories, or blog articles.* These structures are all about a relationship exchange and building trust and credibility. It's about the prospect learning about you and engaging in a relationship, which is different from *getting* something. Sometimes it takes time before they are ready to get something. Take some time to warm them up, educate them, and build trust. You may want to genuinely prove your value and relevance before even trying to make a pitch. In these situations, copy can be less direct or persuasive and more educational.

- *Don't assume you know your audience.* Even if you've been in business a long time, chances are good you don't know your audience as well as you think you do. In my experience, businesses might be correct on *some* things but rarely everything. One little unknown could be a huge discovery in your CRO evolution. This is why it's important to pay attention to your analytics and learn as much as possible about your market's behavior. "Testing before you test" can be a great way to get the information you need.

- *Don't try to be perfect.* This is a huge one. Don't feel like you have to write perfect copy; you're better off putting something down and split testing it. Too many businesses let the search for perfect copy delay the launch of a new site, page, or test. There's always going to be something better, so just put your writing up; then try to improve it. Otherwise, you could be losing money while you wait.

Build Your Skills

The skills lab for this chapter will help you write more persuasive copy, whether it's for a product description, a sales page, an article, or an AdWords ad.

You can find this skills lab at www.ConvertEveryClick.com/chapter7

CHAPTER EIGHT

Video Conversion Strategies

There's something about video that trumps just about every other form of media currently out there. Video allows us a richer experience using more of our senses than just text or audio alone. It's about as close to real life as we can get, at least until holographic video technology gets a little further along. We can see and hear the message clearly, and if it's done well, we can almost smell and taste the sizzling steaks cooking away on that shiny new stove they want to sell us. It's a powerful communication tool and a powerful conversion tool, too.

When it comes to conversion rate optimization, the quantitative and qualitative analytics behind the video are extremely important if you're going to make improvements.

For example, when you host your videos you can track all sorts of viewer data, including what parts of the video they watched, where they stop, where they play, where they replay, and so on. The ability to gather data on how your video is being watched is a key to improving conversions beyond just split testing.

The most popular video hosting platforms include YouTube and Vimeo, but these sites do not yet include the analytical data necessary to make educated conversion improvements. Private solutions like Brightcove and Wistia give you more analytical data to use to help you make decisions about improving conversion. My personal favorite is Wistia, based on their overall value and accessibility to businesses of all sizes. For this chapter, I've asked my friends at Wistia to contribute some of their insights on improving conversions using the data-gathering features of the service.

Conversion Rates with and without Video

In an experiment on Wistia's own pricing page (an area where conversion is obviously a major and direct goal), they wanted to solve the dilemma of people getting confused about exactly what goes into their pricing. People had many questions about how the video hosting plans worked and what exactly bandwidth was, at a time when Wistia was about to automate their bandwidth billing. So it seemed especially important to make things clear.

They put their customer support people in front of a camera to create a couple of videos to demystify video bandwidth consumption and any residual questions regarding their pricing plans. Then their designer went to work recreating the pricing page to accommodate a video while retaining its flow (Figure 8.1).

After the new page went live, it didn't take long to become clear in the numbers that the version with video was driving more conversions.

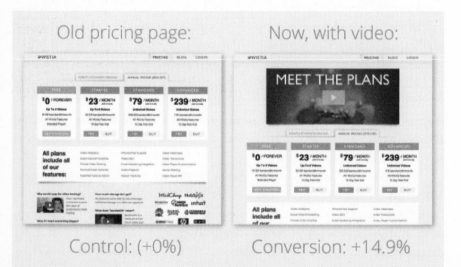

Figure 8.1   **In this split test, Wistia added a video to minimize confusion over their pricing. This proved to increase conversions by 14.9 percent.**

Video Works When You Keep People Engaged

Internet users have long measured the success of their online videos by view count, but what does view count matter if those aren't *good* views? And how can you quantify a *good* view, anyway? Better metrics go beyond the view count. There are several different metrics to analyze a video, two important ones being *engagement* and *play rate*.

Video Engagement

Engagement refers to the percentage of a video that someone watched. An engagement graph (Figure 8.2) shows you how your audience as a whole watched your video, and a heat map allows you to analyze individual viewer sessions (Figure 8.3).

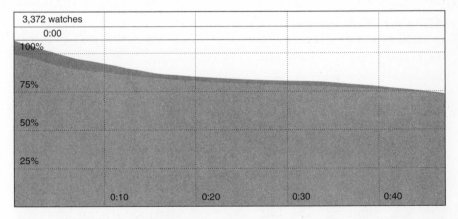

Figure 8.2   This image shows overall engagement throughout the length of the video.

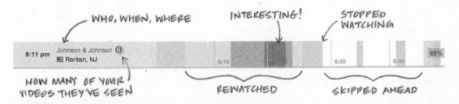

Figure 8.3   This image shows individual engagement in the video and some of the qualitative data it can reveal.

In engagement graphs and heat maps, you can tell where people stopped watching your video and what parts of your video they might have watched more than once. This information can both help you optimize this video and influence how you make more engaging videos for your audience in the future. If you use this data to start split testing video improvements, you will be golden.

In May 2012, Wistia completed a study of the average engagement rates for thousands of business videos of different lengths, and it might prove useful to compare your video with the average (Figures 8.4 and 8.5).

A possible takeaway from these graphs would be to organize the content of your videos journalistically, placing the most important, essential information first and then following with supporting details. It's also probably a good idea to have a hard stop to your video, rather than a meandering ending, if you're planning to use a call to action or e-mail collector at the very end.

Statistically speaking, shorter videos are more engaging than longer videos. With the increased popularity of social media services like Instagram and Vine, which hosts super-short user-contributed videos,

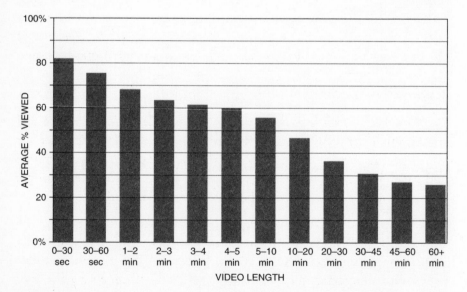

Figure 8.4 This graph shows how long people are watching a video. Data like this can give you insights into the engagement level of your video, and whether you might want to test changing where your important content and calls to action appear.

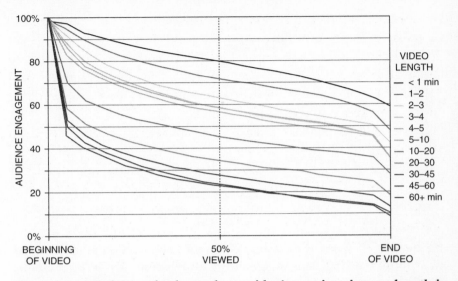

Figure 8.5 **Wistia's study shows that a video's running time or length is important in audience engagement.**

this fact has gone to the extreme. You should strive to make your content as concise as possible to achieve the highest engagement. If your message is more complex, give it the time it deserves. However, understand that a major chunk of your audience won't make it to the end of the video and consider front-loading the most important information.

Video Play Rates

Play rate refers to the percentage of people who viewed your page and started watching your video (see Figure 8.6). Video isn't doing much for you if people aren't playing it. But as always, it depends on your funnel and page plan. If you want them to watch it, how can you entice people to click the Play button? A few possible strategies include:

• *Great thumbnails:* Wistia compared play rates across all Wistia-hosted videos in November 2012 and found that videos with automatically generated thumbnails had an average play rate of 25 percent, but videos with a customized thumbnail (either by choosing a new frame or uploading an image) had a play rate of 34 percent. Although you'll have to do some of your own experimentation to see what works best, a good (albeit rather ambiguous) rule of thumb is to keep it interesting. You're trying to entice people, after all.

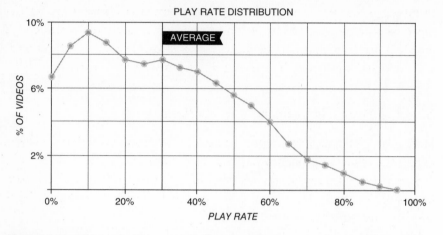

Figure 8.6   Play rate is an example of a microconversion point you may want to be tracking. This image shows distribution of play rates among Wistia users.

- *Location on page:* This seems obvious, but chances are, the more promi-nent your video is on your page, the more likely people are to press Play. This can mean testing your video higher up on the page or mak-ing it larger.
- *Offer context:* Sometimes a little bit of text explaining what purpose the video serves is enough to persuade someone to press Play.
- *Selective autoplay:* When you send people to a video via a thumbnail on another page or an e-mail, you might want to autoplay the video selectively for those people. Although we don't suggest going too crazy with autoplay, in some situations it's a logical follow-up to user behavior.

Video Marketing

One major advantage of looking at statistics beyond view count is that you can figure out how to improve your video marketing over time. Video marketing can be viewed as an iterative process: Create the best content you can, share it with your audience, see how they respond, and react accordingly.

For example, if you publish a video, and the play rate is especially low, consider testing a change to your thumbnail or the placement of the video. If you notice that people are dropping off at a certain point, assess what's going on at that point in the video, and apply those lessons to future videos (or later versions of the same video). If users are watching one part of your video over and over again, are they confused, or did they just love that part of the video? You can learn a lot about your audience and what they like and dislike from your video analytics.

Sharing Your Video with Your Audience

How can you make sure your audience sees your video? We suggest taking a cyclical approach: You create good content, share it with your existing audience, and then they share it with their network. Those new audience members are much more valuable than a random YouTube view because they were referred to you by someone they know.

Video in E-mail Campaigns

Video and e-mail can be the best of friends. As we've talked about, the click-through rate is often the microconversion point with e-mail. Many of my clients have found embedding video in e-mail improves their conversion rates.

In October 2012, Wistia decided to test just how powerful video is for increasing e-mail engagement. They ran a split test using two identical newsletters with similar content, except one had a video as the top piece of content, and the other had an illustrated graphic (Figure 8.7).

The click-to-open ratio (the number of clicks to the number of opens—this factors out any variation in the open rate between the two e-mails, which should have been identical because there was no indication of difference until you opened the e-mail) for the e-mail without a video was 12 percent, but the open rate for the e-mail with video was 38 percent—Wistia saw more than 300 percent improvement.

Although video and e-mail are a great combination in terms of how each can help with the other's success, you still can't embed a video directly in an e-mail message (well, you can certainly put the code there, but chances are it's not going to work with the majority of e-mail clients). The workaround to make sure video in e-mail works for everyone is to create a thumbnail within the e-mail that links to a page where the video is hosted (Figure 8.8).

For the viewers, the experience can be made nearly seamless. When they click a play button in their e-mail, a browser can pop open, and the

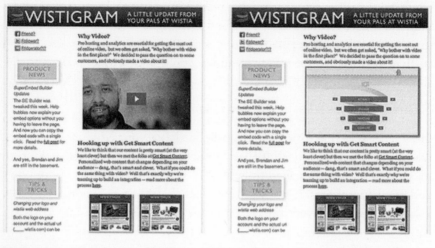

Figure 8.7 This image illustrates Wistia's 2012 split test, which achieved a more than 300 percent improvement just by adding video.

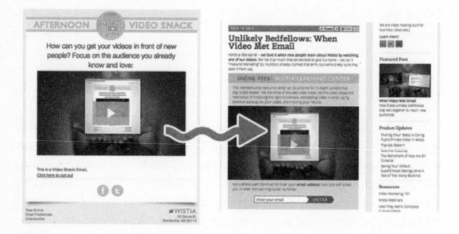

Figure 8.8 While embedding video into e-mail is technically not possible yet, the experience of the workaround solution has its benefits.

video can start playing. (You can use selective autoplay to achieve this.) It sounds a little bit like trickery, but if you try it out for yourself, you'll see that it feels pretty natural.

The good news is that having a video open on your own page has strategic advantages—getting views on your own website is critical strategy-wise, for a number of reasons. I've seen tremendous conversion value in getting people to watch our videos on our clients' websites. It's a similar experience to viewing the video right in the e-mail from the recipient's end, but it gets them into the context of the rest of your content (such as your sign-up forms), something you couldn't pull off with e-mail alone. Video is a great hook that gets people to leave their world of e-mail and enter your world, on your website. You lose some power if the video is just embedded in the e-mail, such as the ability to track the analytics on the video as well as Google Analytics or marketing automation software. And most important, you have more conversion optimization options on a webpage over an e-mail.

With video e-mail services like jiveSYSTEMS.com you can easily add video to your day-to-day communications as well. This can make video a powerful tool for you and your sales team beyond just your marketing efforts.

Driving Direct Conversion with Video

We've talked about how video can be helpful for conversion in more subtle ways, but it can also be used to directly drive conversions. The easiest ways to do this with your videos are *video e-mail collectors* and *calls to action*.

Video E-mail Collectors

Wistia, for example, has its own video e-mail collector tool called Turnstile that links directly to e-mail marketing and marketing automation tools, such as MailChimp, Hubspot, Pardot, Constant Contact, and Campaign Monitor, and it can automatically trigger e-mail drip campaigns or autoresponders when a viewer enters his or her e-mail. Turnstile can be set up at the beginning, middle, or end of a video, and you can give people the option to skip the gate if you want to. Conversion rates can differ depending on where you place your gate, and there are some trade-offs to consider between collecting e-mail addresses and getting as many people as possible to watch the content. Let's start by comparing two of the more extreme use cases.

Wistia collected data from using Turnstile as a mandatory e-mail gate *in front* of their Video Marketing 101 series (a series of videos that served as a basic course on video marketing), as well as from an optional sign-up form at *the end* of the educational videos that they store in their Wistia Learning Center.

For the mandatory e-mail gate, they saw an 11 percent conversion rate over a three-month period. In other words, 11 percent of people who landed on this page submitted their e-mail address and started watching the video. Although they were pretty happy with that conversion rate, it also meant that 89 percent of people who landed on the page were not watching the videos at all because they weren't convinced enough to enter their e-mail address.

For the Learning Center videos, they took the opposite approach and decided to use an optional Turnstile at the end of the video. Instead of a gate, this was more like a call to action asking viewers who made it to the end to sign up for updates. Without a gate up front, these videos had an average play rate of 60 percent but a lower average conversion rate of just 2.3 percent. By using Turnstile at the end of the video, they were able to get more people to watch, but they had to sacrifice the number of e-mail leads.

Requiring viewers to enter their e-mail address to watch your video generally maximizes the number of leads. The trade-off here is the play rate will be decreased. Going this route requires trust from the person landing on that page that your content will be worth giving you their e-mail address. In these cases, try designing the page to give context about your video's content, or use the "e-mail optional" soft gate to encourage viewers to give their e-mail address without restricting access to your content.

With Turnstile, you can also pop up a gate at any point in the video. One way to use this feature is to hook viewers with an introduction so that they're excited to keep watching, and then you introduce a gate. The advantage here is that you can prove your video's value before asking for an e-mail address. The downside is that the interruption may be frustrating to some viewers.

Using Turnstile at the end of your video is the least disruptive to the viewing experience but also the least effective in terms of lead capture. In general, people are reluctant to hand out their e-mail address, so conversion rates are bound to drop when you ask for instead of require one.

The overriding question to consider is, What's the Bottom Line Conversion Rate of a view versus an e-mail address for your business? If an address is substantially more valuable, then the more restrictive the gate the better. But if an e-mail is only marginally more valuable than a regular view, then a soft or optional gate is the way to go. It's totally dependent on context, and the best way to learn is to experiment with your own audience.

In addition to Turnstile, you can get more creative if you have a developer on your side. With some creative code, most video hosting companies will allow you to add your own code to the end of the video. This means you can create your own gate of sorts with a more enticing offer and multiple opt-in fields.

Video Calls to Action

For the most part, people don't add calls to action (CTAs) to video because doing so used to be technically difficult to pull off. Do you add an image to the end of the video? How do you make it an active link? Can you even control what happens at the end of the video (as with YouTube, where the end of the video is outside the scope of what you can customize)?

As a result, most people settle for a simple fade to black or company logo. We've been guilty of that practice ourselves, mostly because it's the easiest thing to do, but this is the perfect time to give your user an idea of what to do next while you've got their attention.

Keep The Get principle in mind when designing your call to action or offer. Here are a few ways you can direct users with a call to action:

- *Free trial or demo:* Once you've shown off a product in a format where the prospect is a passive viewer, why not offer that person the chance to give it a try actively?
- *Contact a sales rep:* Help your users find more information by communicating with a person now that you've scaled the basics of communication to a video.
- *More resources:* Guide your users to the next logical step in learning more about whatever your video is trying to teach or show them.
- *Pricing or buy page:* Direct users straight to pages where they may be likely to convert.

You can track video CTAs in a number of ways:

- URL-shortening services, such as bit.ly, are more than just a way to make messy-looking links prettier. You can also see how many clicks a link is getting from a particular location, and you can compare the number of people finishing the video (from your video's analytics) to the number of people who are clicking your postroll links. Services such as bit.ly are a really easy way to track which paths people are taking to a particular page.

- Urchen Tracking Module (UTM) codes are another, and more technical, tool you can use that are easily trackable in Google Analytics (and you can even combine their power with bit.ly tracking by putting UTM code URLs into bit.ly). You can use Google's URL Builder tool to filter analytics by UTM categories, such as source, medium, and content. For example, if you have a video in a few different places, you can give each postroll URL a different source code. Multiple versions of the same video could be differentiated by varying content codes. An added benefit of using UTM codes with Google Analytics is that you can track beyond just the initial CTA click and keep track of whether people are actually converting by signing up for trials, filling out contact forms, and so on.

Animation: A Great Alternative to Live-Action Videos

One of the big objections to live-action videos is that they are difficult to produce and cost a lot of money. But these obstacles don't have to be true these days—an iPhone records well enough for the Internet. However, there are a lot of other things that need to go into a live-action video, and making one can be really intimidating once you start adding up the costs. If you do a good job, conversions could go up, but it depends a lot on the people in the video, the message they say, how they say it, and lots of other things that can be a bit out of your control.

Fortunately, you do have options. Animation is a great tool you can use to create awesome videos that might convert really well. Animated videos are also cheaper and easier to make than traditional live-action films. Now, I'm not necessarily talking about fancy digital animation like that used for Disney movies, though if you have the skills for that, great! Any instance where a picture moves is an animation—everything from a flip book to talking stick figures on a white board. Businesses are starting to get really creative with how they use animation in video.

Creating videos with animation allows you to design the video exactly the way you want. You have total control over the message, the visuals, and the audio, without ever having to be on camera. Let's look at a couple of easy ways to do this.

If you are thinking to yourself while reading this chapter, "I don't have the resources to make a good enough video" or "I am not good on camera," then an example of a low-cost way to make an animated video. Simply read your web page (the exact, or almost exact copy) into a microphone and then add pictures using a program like PowerPoint, Keynote, or ScreenFlow. You simply make slides like you would for a presentation. Then use the software's record feature to combine the slides with the audio script. This is probably the most inexpensive way to make an effective video.

If you have a little bit more money to spend (anywhere from $1,000 to $20,000 depending on who you hire) you can create an animated video or a cartoon of sorts. This gives your viewers a familiar format and allows you to tell the story in a visual way. If you are selling a product or even a service, some of the best conversion results I have seen come from telling a story through the video. You present the problem and the solution as discussed earlier, but in a context of a story.

I call these the "Meet Bob" videos (Figure 8.9). You've probably seen them on websites before. It's a very simple video that says something like "Meet Bob—Bob has a problem. He wants to take his wife out for dinner tonight, but he's not sure where to go. Fortunately, Bob found The Happy Tummy Restaurant Guide. Now he knows exactly which restaurants are the best in the city." Your company solves Bob's problems. Bob gets to live a happy life and move on. This is a great way to show an example the viewer can relate to that demonstrates exactly how they can use your product or service.

Figure 8.9   Meet Bob videos are a simple and often high-converting way to convey your message.

Another version of a Meet Bob video is called a "whiteboard video." If you have a low budget, this can be a good alternative to more expensive animation. My web development company, ClickCore, started offering these because the demand for good conversion and relatively inexpensive videos was so high with my clients. The basic whiteboard video shows a hand drawing on a whiteboard—just little pictures, phrases, and artwork. The little cartoon characters describe what's being talked about in a fun way, just for the sake of creating a visual to go with the audio message. If you write your audio message well, the whiteboard strategy can be one of the cheapest ways to get things done. My team creates hybrid videos where it appears like a whiteboard video, but is really an animation with the whiteboard style. This allows for easier editing when it comes to split testing changes.

If you can identify your customers and show them a video outlining their problem and the solution they are looking for, and you can do it all in less than two minutes, that's a great start. Animation gives you a cheap and easy way to cut through the resource limitations or imperfections of regular video, and they are much easier to edit if you plan to split test changes.

Using Video Testimonials on Your Website

Any successful business person will tell you how powerful a strong testimonial can be. If you can get your customers to talk *on camera* about how great you are and how helpful your services were for them (with specific examples), it is very much worth testing. There's a special kind of credibility that comes from third-party endorsements where someone else is saying how great you are, rather than you bragging about yourself from a company-centric perspective. Video testimonials are inherently customer-centric.

Television infomercials do a great job of utilizing video testimonials. Are they tacky? Yes, probably, but they convert. It's hard to argue that. People need to see social proof that others have purchased from you, and they are not taking a high risk by being the first to do so. That's why infomercials work; they show other people getting great results using a particular product and they do a great job of showing the problem and solution. You can apply that same logic on a smaller scale with a lot less cost using video testimonials on your web pages and even in places like e-mail.

Common Mistakes to Avoid with Video

- *Don't just wing it.* Write an outline or even a script, if needed. Animated videos especially still require good copywriting even though the words are spoken, not written on a page. Persuasion tactics still apply for video.
- *Don't limit yourself to one style when a mix would convert better.* Animation, live action, screenshots, and PowerPoint recordings are all great forms of communication. Depending on your audience, you may want to vary the ways you communicate through video. Your audience might enjoy different styles, or they might convert really well using one particular method. Testing and tracking your video consumption and conversion rates will tell you where your best options are.
- *Don't forget to split test your videos.* The beauty of having access to video analytics is that you can use the data to split test and optimize your video presentations. Although videos can be trickier to re-create than a landing page or e-mail campaign, the potential for conversion increases is often worth it. Split test your videos just like you would any other web page or campaign change.

Hook Me Up, Benji!

Get access to a FREE Wistia account and a FREE 30-day jiveSYS-TEMS video e-mail account.
Go to www.ConvertEveryClick.com/hookmeup.

CHAPTER NINE

Landing Page Strategies

Meet Bob. Bob uses pay-per-click ads to send people to the product he sells online. When people click on the ad and come to the website, they are pretty much ready to buy and he wants to keep them in that state of mind. He just wants them to click and buy (or more likely, click to opt in). He realizes in his case he's better off without a navigation menu with many unneeded distractions. So a one-page, hyperfocused website makes sense in this case. One-page websites like this are called landing pages. Bob may also have a standard website in addition to this page, or he may have multiple landing pages for different products.

There are many different kinds of websites including hybrid sites, minisites, mobile sites, responsive sites, blogs, and more, but in this book, I am going to focus on the most common four categories. These are landing pages, standard websites, shopping cart sites, and mobile sites (Figure 9.1). So far in this book, you've been learning how Universal Conversion Logic works so that you can make educated improvements no matter what kind of website you have. But there are a few concepts that really are unique to the individual kinds of sites. So, I'm going to spend a brief amount of time discussing these before we move on with traffic, follow-up, and advanced strategies. Just remember as you go

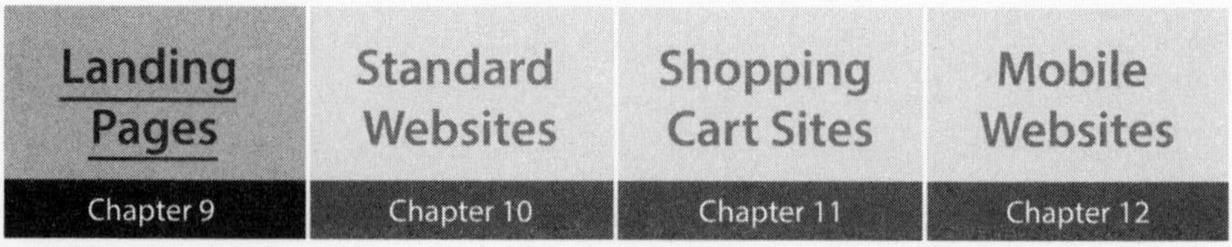

Landing Pages	Standard Websites	Shopping Cart Sites	Mobile Websites
Chapter 9	Chapter 10	Chapter 11	Chapter 12

Figure 9.1

through these next chapters that what you've learned up to now still applies.

Before we start looking at full websites with lots of pages, let's start with the simplest. Landing pages are popular for online marketing because they are effective, relatively quick to create, and very flexible. Technically, a landing page is any page on your website that a visitor lands on after clicking a link, performing a search, or responding to an ad. However, the Internet marketing community adapted this term over time to generally mean any stand-alone page with the only exit link being the main goal. You may also have heard this kind of page referred to as a *squeeze page*. The goal is to squeeze visitors into a funnel or a purchase; they either convert or they don't.

A landing page generally directs the visitor to take one single action and is built for one funnel or purpose. You can think of it as a simple way to create a direct and simple linear funnel website. The desired action transforms an anonymous visitor into a tangible, marketable, qualified lead or customer. Most commonly these days, the requested action is signing up to receive some sort of free information, such as a report, webinar, or e-book. But the goal could also be filling out an interest form, making a purchase, or calling a number to speak with someone. It doesn't really matter what the action is, as long as everything on the page persuades the visitor to convert to that action (Figure 9.2).

When designing a landing page, the Universal Conversion Logic from the design chapter still holds true. In this chapter, we will go over some of the concepts that make landing pages unique.

One of the first concepts to understand about landing pages is that there are many ways to design them. Which way you go all depends on your product or service, your offer, and your goal. There are lead-generating landing pages with simple opt-ins; there are *buy now* landing pages where the goal is to get them to buy in one swift move; and there are landing pages that just pitch something and have a call to action, which takes you to a separate form, page, or website. There are also sub-sets of these, which include video landing pages.

As I said, lead-generating landing pages are becoming more and more common as businesses learn the value of good follow-up marketing. Here's a simple example of that: say you have a landing page that has a purchase as the goal. What happens if they don't purchase? Many times, they are gone and you have lost an opportunity. But if you apply the Double

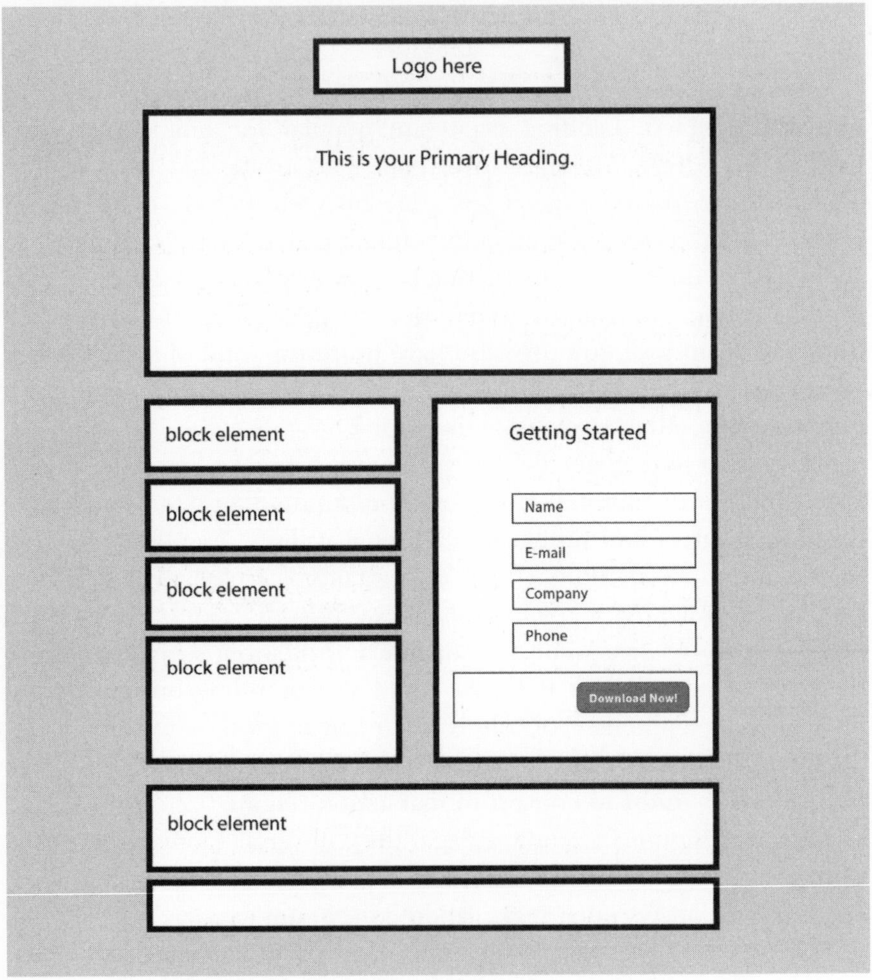

Figure 9.2   This illustration is an example of a traditional lead-capturing landing page layout with an above-the-fold opt-in.

Funnel technique from Chapter 2, you would ask for their contact information first. So, even if they don't buy, you can still follow up with them later. It's all about improving the Bottom Line Conversion Rate.

Short or Long Landing Pages

One of the more common debates with designing landing pages is when to make a page short, to the point, and all above the fold, and when to make it long, where the visitor has to scroll down and read a good amount before a call to action or offer is even made.

Figure 9.3 This is an example of a traditional lead–capturing landing page layout with an above–the–fold opt-in. This example offer and layout should convert well, as long as it passes all three Psychological Conversion Checkpoints.

You've probably come across examples of both of these before. Figure 9.3 shows an example of a basic above-the-fold, or short, landing page. Another example would be a video landing page, which may have a video on the side, an opt-in box, and little or no text at all. Long landing pages histori-cally often have huge headlines, lots of text, and bonus offers, and they usually scroll for a long time. Which style is right for you? Well, only testing can say for sure, but the following are some concepts that may help guide you.

Just like we discussed briefly in the copywriting chapter, short copy and long copy use cases depend on your prospect, your offer, and prod-uct or service. If, for example, someone searches for *cat toys* and they are led to a landing page where the offer is a 100 percent free cat toy or a highly valued consumer guide on the top cat toys, you probably don't need to do much convincing. As long as they can pass the Psychological Conversion Checkpoints (Relevance, Credibility, Value), you can likely get the conversion above the fold. However, if you are trying to sell a higher-end item like a car using a landing page, you will probably need to do more convincing, which will take the rest of the page. That doesn't mean you can't use the Double Funnel technique to market a free consumer guide to get the lead first. But on the sales landing page, you will be hard pressed to sell many cars above the fold.

This is one reason landing pages have been becoming so popular. If you know what you're doing, you can fit a high-quality pitch above the fold with video. Just like we discussed in the video conversion chapter, videos have great benefits in terms of increasing and capturing conversions.

A great way to think about this concept is to ask yourself how long would you need to verbally pitch the offer to a prospect to get a conversion? If it can be done in an elevator ride, above-the-fold will probably suit you. If it will take five minutes or longer to pitch, you may need an extended landing page, video page, or multistep funnel approach over time.

Create Visual Focus

Your conversion point (your goal) is the most important element on your landing page, so make it stand out somehow. We've already talked about visual focus in the chapter on graphic design, but it bears repeating here. Where does the eye go on your landing page? What stands out most? Is it the best element to encourage conversions?

The conversion point could be a big bright button for visitors to click. It could be a phone number to call or a web form to fill out. The design of the page should highlight that conversion point in some way. That might be with obvious elements, such as brightly colored arrows, yellow sticky notes, or videos that play automatically, or the design might call attention in more subtle ways, such as using color and contrast, dividing lines, or layout. The opt-in form can be brighter, or the font can be different. There are lots of ways to draw attention. Testing is really important here to make sure you're using the best method or combination of methods for your audience.

Whether your conversion point is a web form, phone number, or link, it should be one of the first things people pay attention to on the page. The design should draw the eye back to that place over and over again, so that there's no mistaking exactly what you want them to do.

Advanced Strategies

Many of the strategies in Chapter 15 are particularly applicable to landing pages. Just remember, there is no such thing as a one-size-fits-all strategy. The performance of your page will be unique to your prospects, offer, and industry.

Common Mistakes to Avoid with Landing Pages

- *Don't put too much (or too little) information on the page.* Understand where your audience is coming from when they get to the landing page. If they already know they need what you're offering, don't start over and pitch it to them. If they're searching for a printer, they know they need it. You just need to help them see that yours is the best. If they don't know they need the product, or more research is needed to make a decision, you may need to add some educational aspects to the page to help them convert. No matter which you use, long or short page style, split testing is the only way to know for sure you've made the right decisions.
- *Don't think of yourself as your customer.* People who make landing pages tend to build them the way they would respond best. Copywriters can build text-heavy pages; designers can be too picture heavy. Think about your audience and what's going to sell *them*. If you're not sure, test it! Your prospect and customers' intentions measured through conversion rates is how to determine what combination of text, visuals, and video will work best.
- *Don't underestimate the power of a phone number.* People often think they must have an opt-in web form on a landing page. Although that's often the case, you might close more sales with a phone number. It's okay to have two ways to reach the goal on a landing page—a phone call and a web form. Even if the offer is good, and they don't want to call, a phone number can add credibility. Phone sales can be a great way to increase conversion rates on complex or expensive product or service offerings.
- *Don't ignore the psychology behind web forms.* We talked about defining the Ideal Conversion Point back in Chapter 3. If your offer is good and gets as close as possible to the visitor's true desire, you can ask for more information on the web form. Remember this when creating

your landing page offers. Whether the page is making a sale or just collecting information for later marketing, take the time to craft a great
offer and then ask for more information in the web form. You'll need
to test how much information people are willing to give you, but it's
probably more than you think.

- *Don't ignore AdWords quality score and search engine optimization (SEO) on
your landing pages.* Just because you're using a landing page format doesn't
mean you can't enjoy the benefits of good SEO or, similarly, AdWords
quality scores. If you're doing a short above-the-fold pitch, content added
for Google's benefit can be placed below the fold. This placement allows
your landing page to do its job quickly for people who read only above
the fold and keeps Google (and people who read everything) happy with
additional relevant content below the fold. Google ranking and quality
score go up, and cost per click goes down. It's a win-win situation.

- *Don't overlook the logic of foldpages.* It's even more important to remember where the foldpages appear on a landing page. Each foldpage
should have a call to action or offer. There should also be an exit available on each foldpage somewhere, if possible. Keep in mind, the exit
and call to action may be the same.

- *Don't forget international challenges.* Think about who your visitors are,
where they come from, and what might need to be different for them.
A left-to-right layout probably won't convert well in a country that
typically reads right to left. Make sure your layout is consistent with
what they're used to.

- *Don't forget about the power of video.* Videos work well on landing pages
because they appeal to all three online communication styles—text,
audio, and visual in a small space.

  With that said, don't overvalue video either. If visitors are ready to
buy when they get to the page, they may not need a video to convince
them. It may just get in the way of a conversion. Also, creating video
content can be intimidating to some people. Don't let video produc-
tion and perfectionism keep you from launching.

- *Don't use videos without tracking them.* As we discussed in Chapter 8,
using video without tracking user behavior is a big mistake. The data
you can gather is priceless in terms of helping you improve conversion
rates down the line.

- *Don't forget alternative forms of information gathering.* Just because you're
using a landing page doesn't mean web forms are the only way of

gathering information. You can gain insight from geotargeting, tracking, analytics, and so on. These additional insights combined with the web form can make it much easier to lift your bottom line conversion rate.

- *Don't ignore the imagery on your page.* It's important to be careful with pictures. Should the person in the picture look happy or worried? If visitors are looking at a problem-based headline, a worried or sad look could be appropriate. On the other hand, if they're looking at the call to action and people in the image look worried, it could be bad for conversion rates.

- *Don't overplay the fear factor if you don't need to.* The *fear factor* is a technique that emphasizes problems and dangers that might arise if visitors *don't* do what you're asking. It can be powerful in certain circumstances, such as if you are selling home security or tax debt relief. But if your offer is good and people know what they're getting, capitalizing on fear may not be the best-converting tactic. You may not want to remind them of their problems, if they don't need to be reminded. If they already made a decision before they got to your page, just let them convert.

- *Don't force landing pages to stand alone.* Landing pages can work in conjunction with a standard or e-commerce website. They can also consist of more than one page, depending on your needs. We call these mini-sites. Sometimes it takes a bit of testing to figure out the best combination, but there are often great SEO-related benefits to strategies like these.

- *Don't overuse landing pages.* If your product is complicated, is expensive, or requires lots of information and decision making, a landing page might not be enough to get the conversion. In that case, you may want to use the landing page to capture their information and then lead them to a standard web page as a future step in the funnel.

Build Your Skills

The skills lab for this chapter will help you create better landing pages using the seven elements we discussed.

You can find this skills lab at www.ConvertEveryClick.com/chapter9

CHAPTER TEN

Standard Website Strategies

Meet Mary. Mary has a traditional retail store. Someone told her a long time ago that she needed a website, so she had one created. It has a traditional navigation bar, with the usual pages like Home, About, Contact, and so on. But she would like it to bring in more money. Mary has what we call a standard website. When talking about standard sites in this book, I'm referring to websites that are more traditional in nature. They have a typical navigation menu at the top. They might even have a blog attached. Often standard websites couple nicely with landing pages for certain types of campaigns, but let's just stay focused on standard website strategies for this chapter.

Standard websites are sometimes referred to as brochure websites, and there's a reason for that. Standard websites are typically informational in nature. They act like electronic brochures. They generally define a product or a brand, and they may provide some credibility or provide information about products or services. Typically speaking, though, they don't do a great job of selling. As websites became a standard (pun intended), people

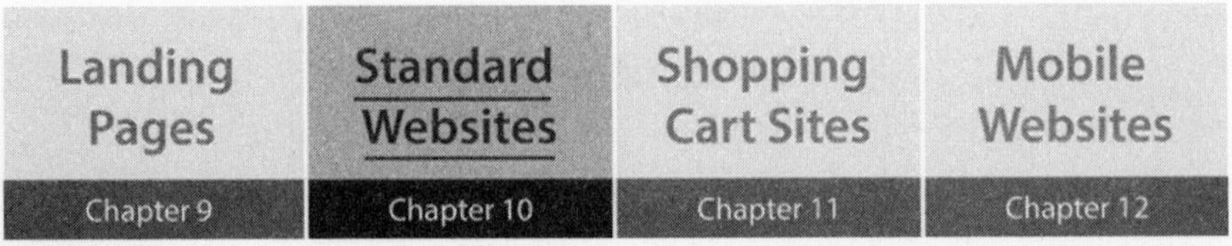

Landing Pages	Standard Websites	Shopping Cart Sites	Mobile Websites
Chapter 9	Chapter 10	Chapter 11	Chapter 12

Figure 10.1

thought it was important to have a website, even though they didn't understand *why* they needed one or what the revenue-generating possibilities were. So web development companies popped up all over the world, offering to build you a website you could be proud of. (Whether they *delivered* on that is another story.) Brochure sites are fine for certain types of businesses where they just need to look legitimate as part of an off-line sales model. But most often it's a better idea to design with conversion in mind.

Brochure websites often miss out on the revenue-generating potential the Internet offers. For years, I have asked prospects and customers, "What's the goal of your website?" I'm looking for them to answer *make money* or *generate leads*. Unfortunately, that's rarely the first answer. Whether you're an Internet or direct-to-consumer company that makes all your money online, or a brick-and-mortar store, or a business-to-business company, your website should work hard to direct as many prospects as possible to make a purchase one way or another.

Standard brochure websites usually do an okay job of presenting information. They talk about the company history and maybe show some pictures of their products or employees. But there's very little talk about *why* someone should buy from that company. What makes it better than a competitor? What's so great about its products or services from a customer-centric perspective?

Brochure websites also typically ignore calls to action and generally lack funnel plans. They assume the visitors will just figure out how to get in touch if they want to buy something. Even adding a simple call to action such as *Come see us today* or *Give us a call* with a phone number can dramatically improve conversions.

Some companies still tell me there's no way to easily access their prospects on the Internet, and it's often business-to-business companies that are most confident in that claim. That's almost never true anymore. There's almost always a way to reach your potential customers through the Internet because almost everyone uses the Internet, even if just for browsing or entertainment. So, there's always a reason to think about conversions and how to optimize them when building your website.

At the end of the day, you will have a more successful business if you create your website in a way that will make you more money or generate more leads. When you start adding in things like calls to action, streamlined navigation, and well-thought-out exit strategies, you move away from a brochure website and toward a higher-converting standard website.

Your Navigation Should Reflect Your Funnel Design

The main navigation is your opportunity to drive the customers to the information you really want them to see. A main, often horizontal, navigation menu is one of the primary features of a standard website. Navigation is often built organically. They start building out page after page after page, giving more and more information about every aspect of the company and what they sell, until the website structure looks like an ant farm—just a giant maze of tunnels (Figure 10.2). Some of the tunnels lead to other tunnels, but many are just dead ends. None of them really seems to be leading anywhere in particular. In other words, there's no end goal. There's no funnel design.

So, you're working along trying to build a pretty website because you think a beautiful site will help add credibility and professionalism to your company. To a certain extent, you're right. It is important to have a professional-looking website for credibility's sake. But as I've mentioned before, some of the best-converting sites I've seen are unattractive to

Figure 10.2 Without good conversion-focused navigation, your website can start to resemble an ant farm, full of winding tunnels and dead ends.

the eye, and some of the most gorgeous sites bomb when it comes to conversions. How can this be? It's because most of the elements of conversion are invisible to the eye, so what the website looks like doesn't really matter. What matters is your funnel design, and how closely your website sticks to that funnel plan.

Building a Strong Page Structure

There are certain pages people expect to see in your main navigation, for example *Home, About,* and *Contact.* The rest is all up to you, with the possible exception of *Contact* because that's often important for a standard website. It's easy to go overboard creating pages, but for higher conversion rates, your page structure depends on what your funnel looks like. You don't want too many extra pages to distract visitors from the path you want them to follow. What do they want to know? Better yet, what do they *need* to know in order to convert? For example, if your website is for a software company, visitors want to know how the software works, how it will help them, how much it costs, and how they can get it. Of course, they need to be able to make it through the Conversion Checkpoints to convert.

Those are the highlights. Those are the steps in the funnel. If you line them up like steps leading to the goal, people will most likely follow along nicely without getting distracted. Not every single page on your site needs to be in the main navigation. It should only contain the elements that are important for conversion. You can still have these pages, but they can go other places on your site, such as the footer, sidebars, or links from other pages. In fact, for most companies I encounter as a consultant, the offer is exponentially more important to a visitor than the *About* page. So, why would we have that in the main navigation? We are often better off finding another place for it, or spreading the content across the site if it's important for the conversion.

Let's take a look at one of my niche software companies, AppointmentCore, as an example. AppointmentCore automates the scheduling process for doctors, sales representatives, consultants, and anyone who needs to make lots of appointments or meetings with prospects or customers. Among other features, it allows prospects to book their own appointments into a calendar and then automatically sets up the conference line call and e-mails the parties all the call-in information.

When designing our website, we needed to start by designing a standard site because that's what people were expecting to see. They needed to see a navigation bar, features pages, pricing, and so on.

Let's forget what we know about conversion for a moment. What would we add for the navigation? Most people would probably add *Home, About, Our Product, Our Customers, Testimonials, Contact,* and pages like that. That's a typical website, and it's not terrible. If we were designing from an SEO perspective, each tab might have about five more pages with drop-down menus under each one, all representing keywords and niches we were targeting.

What's the problem with that? From an SEO perspective, maybe nothing. For conversion, though, the problem is it's information and company-centric instead of conversion and customer-centric. The page structure is focused on the company or SEO only, not the customer and conversion goals. Remember when we talked about the IKEA vs. Walmart floor plans? Think of IKEA as a funnel-focused navigation, and Walmart as more of an SEO-type navigation.

When you optimize a website for conversion, you want it to be as customer-centric as possible. With that in mind, what navigation would we add on a customer-centric website? On the home page, people are going to want to know about the product or service. We may not need an *About* page if we tell about the product or company on the *Home* page. They also may already know who we are depending on how they found us. They are going to want to know how the product works. A *Contact* page is fine, unless we don't want them to contact us. In the case of AppointmentCore, it's a lean sales model, so we'd rather they sign up for a free trial first. And in our case, most people come onto our site relatively educated already, so we put a *Get Started* page in our main navigation instead.

Now let's consider what other things the prospects are looking for. Occasionally there will be visitors who are already customers, and they will need to log in or find support. Therefore, it makes sense to add a log-in section in the navigation or above the fold somewhere. It's probably acceptable if the log-in section is smaller and tucked away in the header. If people are already paying you, they will find their way to the log-in or support page, as long as it's somewhere.

Each of these customer-centric pages has its own funnel leading back to the ultimate goal of signing up for a free trial. We do this because we know the product speaks for itself, so once they try it, they'll most often stick with it.

Define an Exit Strategy for Each Page

Okay, so you've created a navigation bar that follows your funnel plan and shows only your most important calls to action and the pages your visitor needs to see to move to the next step. How do you set up those pages so that people keep following the trail? How do you keep them moving predictably through the funnel?

First, you want the pages to be written in a persuasive manner. Even a basic information page such as How it Works can be written and designed with persuasion in mind. Each page on your website should build a desire in your visitor: a desire to continue on to the next step, regardless of what that is, and a desire to reach the conversion point.

Next, it's really important that each page includes what we call an exit strategy. In the general business world, an exit strategy is typically referring to the way you're going to get out of your business, the end game. For example, in 2011, we built a software company with a very clear exit strategy. We planned to be bought out by another software company for at least seven figures as soon as possible. By the end of 2012, we achieved that goal just as we planned because everything we did focused on that end goal. This made the acquisition an extremely easy proposition for the company that eventually acquired us, and helped speed up the negotiation process.

I'm sure you've heard of the concept that if you set a goal and work backward, you'll figure out a way to achieve the goal. The same works for a website. So, in the case of your website, you want every page to have an exit strategy in mind. You want to lead the visitor through the page and to the next step in the process. It's more than just using a call to action, although that's part of it. You really want the entire page to logically lead the person to take the next step he or she needs to take to reach a conversion point.

For our software program AppointmentCore, the exit strategy for the website is to sign up for a free trial. So all of the pages on the website have several calls to action where the visitor can get started on his or her free trial. The Features page leads to the Pricing page, and so on. Write the information out in such a way that the visitor naturally wants to move on to the next step, and give him or her an obvious way to do that, probably with a button or link. You can't assume people will know what to do next; you have to tell them.

A good general practice is to define each page's call to action differently, because each page is different. It won't feel natural if you're hitting them with the exact same call to action. A natural progression from the home page is to check out the features or learn more about the product or pricing. A natural progression from a pricing page or product description might be to simply sign up or order now. Vary the links and buttons a little. Use different copy in the calls to action. And, of course, these are all just examples, so split test these ideas against variations to see which ones work best.

If you look at most business websites on the Internet today, they don't have this natural progression and exit strategy. This is especially true at the bottom of the page. If your visitors are the kind of people who invest the time to read the whole page, what greets them when they get to the bottom? Most of the time, there's nothing but a generic footer with copyright information and maybe a repeat of the main navigation. I rarely see calls to action above or in the footer, yet something so simple can mean big leaps in conversion rates. Technology is an awesome thing, but people still treat websites like books. Visitors don't have to read one page at a time on a website. They can cut to the chase and flip from page one to the end if they want. Is your product expensive or complex enough that you really need to slow them down to get good Bottom Line Conversion Rates?

Even if you have a brochure website with the sole purpose of convincing the visitor that you are as legitimate as you seem or that a previous purchase or choice was a good one, there's no reason not to have an exit strategy for every page. This is just one simple example of how you can improve a standard website to be more conversion focused. Think of each page as a linear funnel inside your whole website funnel. Each step naturally progresses to the next, but calls to action allow visitors to convert on that particular microconversion in the funnel.

Remember the Fold

The ideas we talked about with the fold line on a landing page also apply to standard websites. Unlike landing pages, though, most standard websites don't have an opt-in web form above the fold. That doesn't mean you *can't* have an opt-in there. If the visitor can easily be convinced to sign up on the spot, it could work there. Generally speaking, though, what people see above the fold on a standard website is what makes them decide whether or not to scroll down or navigate to another page. If a standard website model really is the best option for you, an above-the-fold opt-in on the home page may be premature.

Just keep the fold in mind, and make sure everything visitors see above the fold helps them decide to follow the steps through your funnel. That's why animated sliders and banners have become popular for home pages on standard websites. It gives you a chance to present more than one thing above the fold to have a better chance of engaging them. Whether these banners will work for you depends on what you put on the banners and how you implement them. Again, it's another good time for a split test.

What about Responsive Design?

We're going to talk about responsive design more in Chapter 12, on mobile websites, but I want to bring it up here briefly because it bridges the gap between standard and mobile sites. As you've probably noticed, most people don't browse the Internet on personal computers or laptops exclusively anymore. They use their mobile phones, tablets, game systems, and other electronic devices. Consequently, they are looking at websites on different-sized screens all the time. Websites designed to be responsive automatically read what size screen someone is using and rearrange the content to fit the screen size better. A website will look one way on a laptop, another way on an iPad, and a completely different way on a phone.

If you can get a good handle on responsive design and testing strategies for your standard website, your conversion potential could be exponential. However, don't make the mistake of designing your website as a responsive design website just because it's trendy. Unless you do a good job designing around your funnel, you could actually lower conversions on your mobile website. At the end of the day, you have to decide whether creating a responsive version of a standard website is really worth your time. At the moment, responsive sites are much more complicated to test and track compared to fixed websites. So don't create more work for yourself if there are better opportunities for growth else-where. Think holistically.

Common Mistakes to Avoid with Standard Websites

- *If you're going to build a brochure website for credibility purposes, thinking in terms of conversion can't hurt.* Elements such as calls to action, exit strate-gies, the fold line, and straightforward navigation are still important. They can really help your brochure website be more valuable to your business.
- *Don't be afraid to have a combination of website styles.* It's okay to have more than one website or a combination of styles on separate pages. For example, you may decide to have a standard website but include a few special landing pages. Or you may put an above-the-fold opt-in on your standard website home page, if people are ready to opt in that soon. In that case you are essentially merging landing page principles. It's all about your strategy.
- *Don't forget that many SEO companies and consultants will lead you away from higher conversion rates.* Their goal for a website is typically to rank high on the search engines, not to get more conversions. For SEO, content is king. They will often want to create too many pages, add too much distracting content or links in the main navigation, include more exit links and over-optimized keywords, and so on. Although SEO is a powerful tool, you want to find a happy medium or a work-around. Sometimes that can be as simple as having a separate website for SEO or putting most of the content below the fold (leaving the space above the fold clean and uncluttered).
- *Don't put unnecessary things in navigation.* Too often people feel the need to add lots of pages in their navigation. Remember, your naviga-tion should reflect your funnel plan. Keep it simple and easy to follow. For example, if your SEO person told you to write a blog for SEO purposes only, you probably shouldn't have it highlighted in the main navigation. It's a distraction unless you really want people to read it for conversion purposes as part of your conversion funnel plan.
- *Don't make it hard to find you.* If you're making a brochure website, add your phone number and contact page in a prime location. Make con-tact information very easy to find. People are going to want to know

how to contact you. The only exception is if you can't (or don't want to) support the volume of support calls that produces.

- *Don't waste space above the fold*. Every business loves its logo and branding, but too often people waste space in the header. Although branding is important, it shouldn't take up a quarter of the screen. You need room to put your most valuable content above the fold. If your header takes up all the room, there's probably great room to optimize.

- *Don't forget the visitors' natural reading direction*. If the website is in English, people will read naturally from left to right. If you are targeting a country with a right-to-left language, consider that in your design plans.

- *Don't overthink your website so that it delays your launch*. Standard websites tend to take a long time to complete. You're better off with a new conversion-focused website that's *almost* perfect than an old website that does a terrible job of converting and proving credibility. Unless you're a huge company where everything you do makes the news due to sheer traffic volume—then launch, test, and tweak. Opportunity cost is a real thing.

- *Don't include social media icons in the header, unless they're absolutely necessary*. This is one trend that drove me crazy. People use these icons in their header mostly because someone told them how important social media integration was on their website. There's no value in having these icons above the fold *unless* you're really focused on a high-quality social media presence or if these icons show credibility immediately through a large count of followers as part of the icon. If you have great content, great community, awesome engagement, or if you have a blog that is intended to capitalize on social media, then you can show the icons in a prime location. Otherwise, I would just keep that information in the footer.

- *Don't hire a web designer who does't design with conversion in mind*. As we discussed in the graphic design chapter, most web development companies out there actually build websites for their clients, not for their clients' customers. That's a very important distinction. They design to make the client (you) happy, not to make you money. They will give you what you want to see, not what your *prospects* need to see to become customers. It's not on purpose, and they probably don't even realize that's what they're doing. Generally, that means everyone loves how the website looks. It's so pretty. It's so hip. It's so progressive. Uh-huh. That's nice. What you need to know is, does it convert? Does it convert better than the old site? Or, how can we make it convert better? So, when you go looking for designers, pay attention to the kinds of questions they ask. See if they mention ROI or conversion at all. If they don't, go ahead and ask some questions about it. Find out if they test to make sure the new website converts better than the old website. If they have to "look into that," it's probably not part of their business model. Ask them what their other clients' ROI has been. You're probably going to get blank stares. In which case, keep looking (unless conversion isn't really important to you)!

Build Your Skills

The skills lab for this chapter will help you match your navigation to your funnel and design exit strategies for your pages.

    You can find this skills lab at www.ConvertEveryClick.com/chapter10

CHAPTER ELEVEN

Shopping Cart Website Strategies

Meet Larry. Larry has a brick-and-mortar store, but he also wants his customers to have the option to shop online. So, he hired a designer to build an electronic version of his real-world store and set up a checkout system so they can browse and buy online without leaving their homes.

The third common website type is the e-commerce site, online store, or shopping cart model just like what Larry wanted to build (Figure 11.1). Just so we're all on the same page, let me explain what I mean when I talk about a shopping cart model. You can think of this as an online store. The name implies that it has a shopping cart. Over time, the terms *online store, e-commerce site*, and *shopping cart site* have all become interchangeable. I'm sure you've heard other names for them as well. In the context of this chapter, these websites are like online catalogs, where people can browse through products and categories, add things to their virtual cart, and check out when they're ready to complete a purchase. Standard websites and landing pages can use shopping cart technology, too, so some of the concepts discussed in this chapter apply to those websites as well. Back in 1999, I developed my first online store

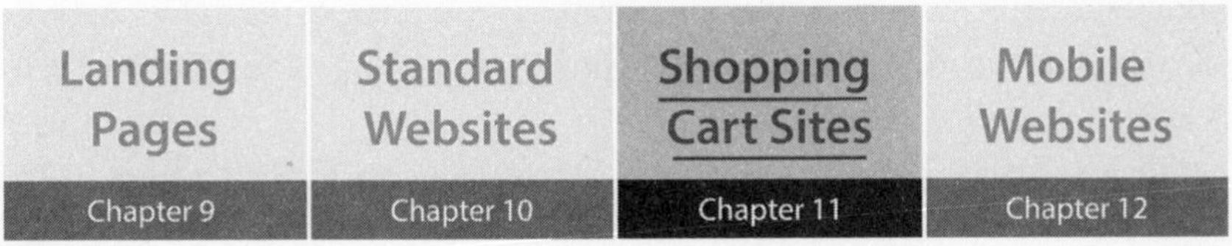

Landing Pages	Standard Websites	Shopping Cart Sites	Mobile Websites
Chapter 9	Chapter 10	Chapter 11	Chapter 12

Figure 11.1

for a client. It was just a simple catalog of products coded from scratch with add-to-cart buttons for the cart and checkout. These days most e-commerce is based on shopping cart software, which often includes the storefront, shopping cart, and checkout tools.

When it comes to shopping cart websites, usability practices are often directly related to getting better conversions. You want to make the path to the checkout as fast and easy to follow as you possibly can. Generally, the more you deviate and get creative with shopping carts and user interface innovations, the more conversion rates will go down.

Unlike other chapters where we discussed Universal Conversion Logic (UCL) and the psychology behind what might improve conversion rates, a lot of what we're going to talk about in this chapter falls in the realm of usability. The goal is to help people find what they're looking for and make purchases quickly. In the case of shopping carts, the UCL is about giving people what they expect or what they're used to and making it as easy as possible to find it and then make a decision to purchase. Let's start by looking at what people typically expect and therefore need with navigation design in order to convert.

Navigation

When you go to your favorite grocery store, you have a pretty good idea how to navigate it, right? Even if you've never been in a store before, you could probably find everything on your list if it were well laid out; it would just take a little more time. Each aisle is usually marked with categories to help you find the items faster. Occasionally, you might get lost, but most stores keep things in similar sections as other stores. The best ones make it easy to find things. You've probably also been to stores where there were aisles and categories, but you still couldn't find what you wanted.

Both of these stores have certain things in common. They both have aisles and categories, but they aren't equally effective. The best stores make navigating intuitive. Items are where you expect them to be. In the less successful stores it's difficult to find exactly what you're looking for. It's very frustrating, right?

That's what it's like when a stranger comes to a typical, unoptimized shopping cart website for the first time. It's like shopping in a new store that's poorly laid out. They have no clue where to look for what they want. Confusing buttons direct them off the path, items are labeled strangely, the categories are weird, nothing is where you'd think, and the whole website seems to be written in a different language. It's easier for the visitors to just click away and find a different (easier to navigate) website that offers what they're looking for. In a brick-and-mortar store, there's a significant time investment involved in walking around the store and filling up a cart. People are less likely to simply abandon a cart in the aisle and go look someplace else. But it's different with online shopping. Visitors didn't have to drive to your store or spend time physically adding items to their cart. No one will notice if they just abandon the cart. They are anonymous, and they are only one click away from abandoning your website completely. That's why it's so important to optimize your shopping cart to reduce any friction for the user.

Ideally, your website should feel familiar. The goal is to make visitors feel right at home as fast as possible. You want to make it easy to find exactly what they're looking for. A good navigation structure will help your credibility and relevance by creating a professional and trustworthy feel to the overall website. This is subtle, but the effects on your conversion rates are real. In general, the more you try to reinvent the online shopping cart, the more difficult it will be to use and the lower your conversion rates will be. Here are some ways to improve your shopping cart websites for better conversion rates.

- *Stay focused.* On product pages and descriptions, don't give visitors anything to distract them from the Add to Cart or Order button. Many companies clutter up their product pages with links to other products or even other websites and ads. Once visitors click away, they probably won't be back. (Unless you're Amazon.com—then you're the exception, not the rule.)
- *Be specific.* Don't use confusing names in navigation, categories, or products themselves. You might think a navigation button to *The Runway* is a clever way to say *Gallery* on a clothing boutique website. But many visitors might not get it, and they might not take the time to figure it out. Likewise, try not to have confusing category names. If visitors come to your website to buy a shovel, don't make them figure out the difference between landscaping supplies, garden essentials, and outdoor tools.
- *Don't be creative.* For these websites, think *inside* the box. Things need to be as plain and familiar as possible. For example, put your navigation bar exactly where people expect to find it.

- *Be redundant.* Put items in multiple categories so that people can find them. There's no law that says you're only allowed one category per product. You're the boss of your website. List that shovel in landscaping supplies, garden essentials, *and* outdoor tools.
- *Organize lists.* Most people dislike sorting through long lists of random items. Help them find what they need by breaking down long lists into sublists. You can also alphabetize long lists using the most common vocabulary, or try adding *best seller* or *most popular* icons where appropriate.

Associated Products and Upsells

With shopping carts, conversions do not stop with the individual conversion. It's all about getting your revenue per order and returning customer numbers higher. A common mistake I see is when people try to make their product pages too concise, almost like a landing page, where there are no exit links or other opportunities. That approach might get the initial purchase, but it loses the opportunity to get the customer to spend more money on the order. That's why stores such as Walmart put all the fun, cool products at the ends of the aisles and place enticing and high-margin items in the checkout lines. They want you to spend more per visit. Sometimes supermarkets put ping pong balls in the beer aisle. Why would they do that? Because ping pong balls are also used in beer pong, and it's an associated upsell product.

Amazon.com has made a fortune offering additional products to customers purchasing and browsing on its website. More and more websites are using this as a way to encourage you to revisit products you've looked at before or to check out something entirely new in a similar category. This is another customer-centric conversion technique. It's a way to make the website seem more tailored to visitors and what they're looking for.

Another more common conversion technique is using product-centric versions of recommended products. Have you ever seen a related products section on your favorite e-commerce website? Product-centric cross-promotion happens when you add a product to your shopping cart, and the website recommends other accessories or related products to you. For example, if you buy a cell phone online, the cart might show you pictures of a wall charger, a car charger, or spare batteries in a section marked "related products."

You might also cross-promote with recommended products. A good example of this is when Amazon says, "People who bought product X also bought these." Maybe you bought a *Star Wars* DVD, and the website recommends other DVDs in the science fiction genre. With this technique, you're grouping certain things in an effort to either upsell additional products or help the visitor explore deeper in the category. This can backfire, though, if you offer too many choices or if people get lost and can't find their way back to the original interesting product. So remember to test any changes you make to be sure you're helping and not harming sales.

Shopping Cart Abandonment

People are notorious for changing their minds. They will fill up a shopping cart with lots of cool stuff and then just click away without making the final purchase. This is commonly called cart abandonment, and it's one of the biggest problems e-commerce sites face. There are many reasons people do this.

Often people abandon for usability reasons, or they were put into the decision-making mode too many times. You want to make the decision process as easy and seamless as possible. This is one of those examples where usability and CRO overlap. If the process is difficult, time-consuming, or overwhelming for someone, it only takes a half second to click and leave the store.

If visitors filled their cart and then got distracted by a phone call or realized they didn't have their wallet handy, there's not much you can do. But most times there are steps you can take to help more people complete the transaction. Here are some ways you can reduce cart abandonment and improve your bottom line conversion rate.

- *Where are they leaving?* The first thing you need to find out is where you're losing people. Is it on the checkout page or the credit card form? Are they even able to find the checkout? Once you pinpoint the trouble spots, it's easier to make meaningful improvements.
- *Use more than one touch.* Remember from the graphic design chapter how it's often a good idea to have a call to action on every foldpage? Well, the same concept applies to shopping carts. People often need to see things more than once. For example, they might not notice the checkout button in your header, so you might also put it at the bottom of the page if they scroll below the first foldpage. Also, you might want

to consider a perpetual cart—which is a running subtotal of items in the cart.

Perpetual carts are popular on larger retail websites, such as Amazon. They are often located in more than one location and have a clear way to proceed to the checkout.

- *Give directions.* No one likes getting lost. Imagine your website is like a dark highway. People need road signs to tell them where to go and what to do. Drivers appreciate plenty of warning before an exit and big arrows pointing the way. Shoppers appreciate clear directions, too. For example, you could use arrows or colors to help your calls to action stand out. The graphic design principle of weighting your most important elements applies here. However, don't have too many competing calls to action. Shopping carts often have lots of features, such as edit cart, remove item, continue shopping, recalculate/update, and so on. So make sure the main call to action, such as, "Proceed to checkout," stands out clearly.

- *Keep them safe.* Visitors want to know it's safe to shop with you. It's part of the *credibility* Conversion Checkpoint. Elements such as a secure shopping cart, a no-hassle return policy or money-back guarantee, testimonials, and trust logos all help the visitors know they are in a secure environment, as long as they feel credible. But don't overdo it. If you met a questionable salesperson wearing 10 badges of all the awards he'd won, you might wonder about how real the awards were. Sometimes a little modesty does help credibility.

- *Remember reading order.* If your visitors' language means they normally read left to right, they will automatically expect to enter a page's content on the left and exit the page on the right. So it usually makes sense to put Add to Cart buttons toward the right side of the page. You can also add other credibility and trust elements, such as your phone number, to the right-hand column. If your visitors will be reading right to left, such as with Hebrew or Arabic, exit and trust elements may work better on the left side of the page.

- *Test your in-cart upsells.* Upsells are typically done after the checkout process, but you can also present these opportunities before that. Upselling can dramatically increase your revenue. But depending on your market and how you present the upsell, it can also lead to cart abandonment. You don't want to appear pushy or annoying, but you also don't want to be too soft and miss out on potential extra sales. Split testing is really the best way to tell if you're striking the right balance. Just make sure you are measuring the micro- and bottom line conversion rates.

- *Have a guest checkout.* Remember from the information capture chapter that people don't like to be forced into creating an account. If the offer is there, they may *choose* to register, but it's best to give them the guest option. Sometimes people just want to check out quickly, and a guest checkout is the better option.

- *Use coupons and promo codes carefully.* Using coupons can be a double-edged sword on e-commerce websites. On one hand, if you have a coupon field in your checkout, people may feel like they're getting a deal. On the other hand, if they don't already have a code handy, they may leave your website to go find the best value. They may get frustrated as they try expired codes or find conflicting information, or they might get distracted and not come back at all.

  If coupons aren't a part of your sales process, it might be worth testing leaving that field off your checkout form. If you do want to offer these discounts, make sure they are easy to find right on the website (or right on that page). You might even consider filling in the discount code for them as a surprise or if they try to leave your site. Imagine how delighted they will feel when they get unexpected value. That goodwill can go a long way when asking for referrals or social media sharing. If done right, it can significantly improve your cart abandonment issues.

- *Disclose the full price up front.* People will sometimes abandon a cart because of hidden charges. Even though charges such as tax and shipping are expected, if you don't tell people the full price, they can develop a negative feeling. Try to calculate all the charges and arrive at a final price before they get to the later stages of the checkout process. This way they know exactly what they're paying when they get to those critical final steps and they will be less likely to leave.

- *Bring them back.* If you take the time to capture visitors' e-mail addresses at the beginning of their visit, or as part of your Double Funnel strategy, you have the ability to bring them back. If possible, identify visitors as early as possible. Then when they return to your website, you can give them a friendly message welcoming them back and reminding them they still have items in their cart. With a sophisticated web team, you can even track what they're interested in with cookies and attach that data to an e-mail address. Large enterprise e-mail marketing tools, such as Eloqua, allow for this right out of the box.

Common Mistakes to Avoid with Shopping Cart Websites

- *Remember, don't be creative.* I can't tell you the number of people who have asked for a drag-and-drop system to place items into the shopping cart. They want to provide a creative shopping experience, which is fine in theory, but there's an educational issue. People expect Add to Cart buttons and checkout pages. They don't know how to interact with anything too creative. If they can't figure out how to work the system, they're just going to abandon it.

- *Don't forget to test different checkout processes.* Figure out how to make the entire process easier for the user. You might try a multistep, accordion-style, smooth-capture (as we'll discuss in Chapter 15), or single-page checkout process. (An accordion-style checkout just means that each step expands as you complete the step before it.) There are also different ways to present step indicators. Different audiences are going to react differently to the various techniques.

- *Don't assume fewer steps are better.* People often think one-step checkouts are better for conversion rates, but I've seen many cases where that is not the case because the process is too overwhelming. One-step checkouts are fine if you don't have a lot of information to collect. But if your process is long, as we discussed with long-capture forms, you're better off tweaking an accordion, a smooth-capture, or a traditional multistep process.

CHAPTER TWELVE

Mobile Website Strategies

Over the past few years, the lines between computers, televisions, phones, game systems, and other computing devices such as tablets have been permanently blurred. There's no getting away from it. People are visiting websites more and more often on alternative devices. Web browsing has become a personal experience from the consumer's perspective. Unfortunately, the websites themselves still seem stuck in the days when everyone used more or less the same platform. Standard personal computers haven't disappeared, but if you're thinking about maximizing conversion rates, it's important to think about whether you need a mobile conversion plan.

In Chapter 7 we talked about the idea that the best conversions come from customer-centric design plans. In an ideal world the customer's experience would be totally individualized to him or her. Of course, that's not 100 percent possible (at least not yet), but we want to get as close to a personalized experience as we can. One of the attributes of a customer-centric model is the individual screen size and device type. After all, people interact with websites differently depending on how large or small their screen is, and whether they use a mouse or their finger.

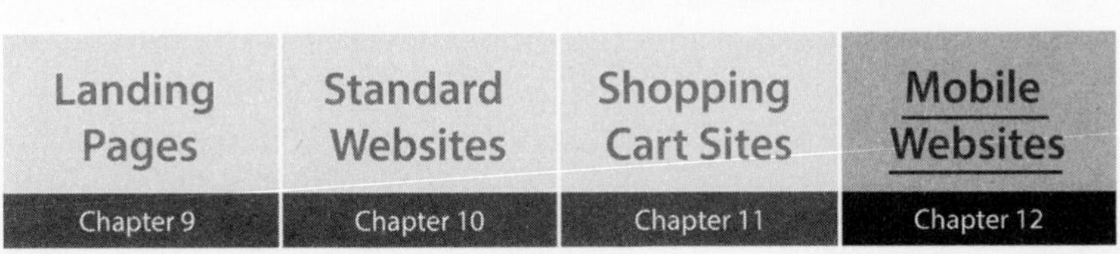

Landing Pages	Standard Websites	Shopping Cart Sites	Mobile Websites
Chapter 9	Chapter 10	Chapter 11	Chapter 12

Figure 12.1

In this chapter, I'm going to talk mostly about mobile devices in terms of phones, rather than tablets or personal game devices. Just remember these other tools are often considered mobile devices, too.

How Usability Plays a Role in Mobile Conversion

When visitors come to a website from a computer, they're expecting a certain user experience. As we've learned in previous chapters, you don't necessarily have to give them that experience. But you can define a better *converting* experience, give them more of what you want them to see, and lead them toward the Ideal Conversion Point, where your desire and their desires intersect.

When people visit your website from mobile devices, however, their experience is going to be different from website to website. Their setting and intentions are different, too. In the past, you pretty much knew visitors were either on a home computer or a computer at work. These days, you have no idea where they are or what distractions may be present. Are they in a car, surrounded by hungry kids, desperately seeking the nearest burger joint? Or are they taking a few precious minutes of downtime between meetings to look you up? Or are they accustomed to using their phones for almost everything?

Most businesses still don't have a stand-alone mobile website or even a mobile version of their website. They count on the fact that a phone will automatically shrink a regular website down so that it fits. Of course, it doesn't really fit. More often than not, they don't think about it at all because it's not really on their radar. The website is so small on the phone's screen that the person must zoom in and zoom out just to see and navigate the page.

As mobile usage has increased, I have seen more companies starting to make separate mobile websites. They've heard it's the new cool thing to do, and it is. Unfortunately, most developers building mobile websites don't keep the funnel in mind. The mobile versions are built to serve as minisites or, worse, just smaller versions of regular websites.

On a regular website, you can use links, pictures, buttons, and all sorts of things to navigate through the website. But on a mobile device, the mobile design standards say you should really stick with clickable menu buttons to move from page to page. Typically, people think the whole website should be a series of navigation, buttonlike links, and short paragraphs of information. The more straightforward the information, the better. What they are describing is a good brochure-style website with information about your services or location. Just like standard brochure websites, this doesn't take into account a strong funnel plan. I often have to ask, "Do you want to build an informational website, or do you want a website that converts?"

Make the Goal Easy to Find—Really Easy

Sadly, most of the mobile websites I see out there don't include calls to action at all. It's almost as if they chucked return on investment (ROI) right out the window when creating the mobile website. This is why a regular website shrunk down by the mobile device surprisingly often converts better than professionally designed mobile websites. It's as if we're back in the early days of the Internet again, when just having a website was all that mattered. Having a cool website was all that was really important, whether or not it made any money. Unfortunately, this is still pretty typical today.

The mobile experience is still relatively new, and most companies just don't know what they're doing in that realm. They listen to their web person or design advisors, who say they "need a mobile website. Mobile websites are in! They're cool! You gotta get one." Everyone's flocking to create a mobile website just for the hell of it. As long as it looks halfway decent on the boss's iPhone, it's all good. How is that good?

Don't be one of those companies. When building your mobile website, think carefully about your funnel. Think about how people will interact with your mobile website. What do they want most? Where are they coming from? Where is the Ideal Conversion Point? Because the audience's behavioral context (their setting, intention, and actions) is different on mobile, your mobile website needs to look and run differently, too.

Do You Really Need a Mobile Website?

As we discussed in the data gathering chapter, tools such as Google Analytics let you see how many people are coming to your website from mobile devices and what ones they're using (or at least the browser version of the mobile devices). If you look at that number and think to yourself, *if I can get a few percentage points more of those people to convert, I could make a lot more money*, then the ROI is probably right for you to focus on mobile.

If you don't have much mobile traffic right now, ask yourself "am I missing something?" Is there traffic out there that you should be getting? With advertising networks, such as Google AdWords, you can specifically target ads to mobile users only. There may be enough people out there using mobile devices to find companies like yours to make targeting mobile traffic worth your while. If so, you may want to consider buying some mobile traffic.

No matter what data you find, keep in mind that mobile usage is growing every day. Even if your data says you don't need a mobile website right now, you should keep it in mind for the future. It's inevitable that a mobile website will be worth your while at some point, whether now or in the near future.

Responsive Design Is Becoming More Common

As I mentioned, there are many screen sizes and devices. The experiences on the large and medium screen sizes are fairly similar, but when you get to the smaller phone screens, you really have to rethink your funnel a bit. Most mobile devices are already capable of miniaturizing a regular website to be viewable on a smaller screen. Unfortunately, those minisites aren't very user-friendly. You have to scroll around and maximize parts of the screen, and clicking links can be a real challenge. Fortunately, responsive web design is becoming more and more common. When a website is responsive, that means it automatically figures out what size screen the visitor is using. Once it knows that critical bit of information, it uses flexible images and grids to resize the website to fit the screen properly.

The more common responsive design becomes, the more people are going to expect your website to fit their screen size. Sooner or later, you're probably going to want to make your website responsive.

Some Basics to Consider When Building Your Mobile Website

The bigger the size of your company and the more visitors you have, the more likely your mobile website audience is important and has a valid ROI. As the months and years roll by, more and more people are going to visit your website on mobile devices. Building a basic mobile website with a simple conversion funnel may help you get ahead of your competitors at first.

But the more mobile volume you have, the more your mobile website funnels should have parallels to your regular website. For example, rather than having small menus with little paragraphs of information on your mobile website, it might be better to simulate your landing page with a really clear call to action to have visitors call or opt in. Over time, you may want to develop your website to closely follow your regular website funnel. It's simplified for mobile, but it parallels the way your regular website looks and feels. This is why responsive will become a future standard. It's the underlying philosophy. It's less about beauty and more about function. Here are a few things to keep in mind:

1. *Consider users' settings and intentions.* If people are browsing your website on a mobile device, where are they likely to be? At home or traveling? What information are they most likely looking for? How can you make that information really easy to find? Where are they coming from? Did they search for you on Google? Did they click an ad? The answers to these questions can give clues to their intentions.

2. *Consider your funnel.* How can you move visitors to their conversion point as quickly as possible? (It's probably simpler than you think.) Universal Conversion Logic principles still apply for mobile. Do you have a long sales process, where you're better off collecting their information and continuing the conversation over e-mail, or are they ready to call and buy? If they have their phone in hand, they may be ready to just call.

3. *Add calls to action.* What do you want site visitors to do? Call you? Opt in? Click a button? Make it clear exactly where and how to do it. Remember, they are on a tiny screen. They may have really big fingers. Don't make them dial; add a call button or at least make your phone number clickable. Don't make them type in lots of information; use short capture forms and keep them as short as you can.

Don't overthink it. The conversion logic principles discussed in the previous chapters are mostly applicable to mobile devices. The big difference is that the smaller the screen, the less left-to–right logic applies because the screen is too small. Exit tabs will often be in the center or full width of the screen because there really isn't a left and right.

Just keep in mind that the user experience on a mobile device is expected to be different from the user experience on a regular computer, mostly because there isn't enough room and the majority of mobile Internet speeds aren't fast enough just yet. The screens are significantly smaller, and people spend even less time on a mobile website than on a regular website. So your funnel should be as straightforward as possible.

How to Use Call Buttons Effectively

Imagine you're sitting in a hotel room in an unfamiliar city and you're craving a pizza. You look up local pizza delivery on your phone. Do you want to spend time waiting for slow-loading pictures, reading useless "welcome to our website" messages, or scrolling all over the website to find what you need? No. Of course not.

What do you want? A phone number. That's all. Just a simple phone number. It's not too much to ask, yet so many mobile websites make it difficult to find the one piece of information most mobile searchers want.

Depending on your business model, you may or may not want someone to call you. For example, one of my companies is a service company, and we encourage people to call us. Another company is a products company, and we prefer they just sign up on the website. So, if you have a business where you *do* want people to call you, then this section will be useful for you.

A good way to get started optimizing a mobile website is to make sure that your home page has a prominently displayed phone number or a call button (Figure 12.2).

It depends on the business, of course, but people navigating from a phone are looking for your phone number to call you. You don't want to miss out on those opportunities right out of the gate. Click-to-call buttons are buttons coded into a mobile website. When clicked, it enters the correct phone number into the person's phone for them so that he or she can call you without typing the numbers. Coding a call link is very similar to coding a regular hyperlink: <ahref= "tel:8005550000">800-555-0000</a>, where you replace the example phone number with the number you want users to call.

Figure 12.2 Sometimes all people really want is basic information like a phone number or an address. Don't make your site more complicated than it needs to be.

We ran a click-to-call button test recently for one of my larger Fortune 500 conversion-consulting clients. We looked at one of the landing pages I thought needed a mobile version. The client's current mobile page was focused on the promotion it was offering. By simply changing the focus to a phone number with a call button above the fold, the client started receiving more calls. The company increased sales conversions by more than 30 percent immediately. The whole change could have been done for a small business for a few hundred dollars. It was a negligible cost for the larger company, and there was a significant return on investment.

Web Forms Need to Be Simpler, Too

If you have landing pages or websites where an opt-in web form is part of your funnel, make sure the form is easy to fill out. A long, detailed contact form, for example, is extremely difficult to type out on a mobile phone. You're often better off just asking them for a first name and an e-mail address or phone number to get them started. You could have someone call them back to collect more information, or you could use the e-mail address to follow up with them later. Don't forget about texting information, too. These strategies sound logical, but they're very rarely used because the business world has been so slow to respond to the increasing use of mobile devices.

Common Mistakes to Avoid with Mobile Websites

- *Don't assume your audience is (or isn't) using mobile.* This is probably the biggest mistake. Whether you use mobile or not, your target market probably does, or at least a segment of it does; that segment is growing every year. If you need numbers to prove this, check out your Google Analytics. The data will tell you exactly how many people are trying to view your website on mobile. Use that to decide what to do.
- *Don't forget mobile means more than just phones.* Tablets and gaming devices keep people connected to the Internet as well. When you build your funnel and your website, consider all the places and situations people might be viewing from. Then make it as easy as possible for them to get to the conversion point. Fortunately, tablets are big enough that people can often get away with using their regular sites.
- *Don't make it complicated!* Depending on your business, your mobile website could be as simple as one page with a paragraph of text and a call button. Remember the Plinko® problem? You want them to slide straight down the funnel, with little or no bouncing around.
- *Don't forget to add calls to action above the fold and on every page.* Your calls to action are the most important thing on your mobile website. Make them clear, plentiful, and easy to use.
- *Don't forget where e-mail fits in the overall picture.* When you communicate with prospects and customers using e-mail marketing, remember people may be checking their mail on a mobile device. The pitfalls of reading e-mail on a phone are the same as reading a website on a phone—no one wants to wait for pictures to load or to scroll through miles of meaningless text to find a call to action. Keep your e-mails optimized for reading quickly on mobile devices.

- *Don't forget there are different expectations for different operating systems.* This means Android versus iPhone versus iPad versus Android tablets versus whatever is coming next—not to mention all the different sizes of phones and tablets out there. Different platform users have different expectations and standards. For example, there are lots of Android phones out there and they're all different sizes. Even iPhones are entering into a multiple-screen-size model.

  If your audience is large enough, it might be worth considering designing separate funnels for different platforms. As I mentioned previously in the chapter on graphic design, this is partly what responsive design is all about if you are using it for conversion rate optimization. It's how I like to define truly responsive mobile design, responding to the people, where they're coming from, and what they're thinking, not just the size of their screen.

- *Don't forget about mobile commerce.* In the early days of the Internet, people were afraid to enter their credit card information into a website. It took a long while for e-commerce to really take off, but these days, most people feel safer using an online order form than a paper one. The same thing is happening with mobile commerce. As banks start offering mobile commerce apps, and people get used to shopping right on their phones, mobile commerce will become more widely adopted. If you take orders online or have a shopping cart website, think about your visitors' experience when they check out on their phones. This is another great reason to encourage your shopping cart users to make an account and save a credit card on file. From their phone, all they need is their e-mail and password to make an order, which is less daunting than typing a credit card number into the phone.

CHAPTER THIRTEEN

How to Optimize Traffic for Conversion

Before anyone gets to your website, they have to find it. In the timeline model of Holistic Conversion Rate Optimization (HCRO), optimizing traffic happens *before* people get to your website, and it is just as important to your bottom line conversion rates as what happens while they're there. Ideally, you want the most targeted traffic you can get. Then you should have alignment all the way down your linear conversion funnel. The traffic should be aligned with the website, and all the way down through the follow-up. Each step in the funnel should be created as a continuation of the previous step. It's about lining up the pins on the Plinko® board, as we discussed in Chapter 2.

Traffic optimization is the science of increasing conversions and lowering the cost, most often to allow for more volume and growth. When it comes to traffic, conversions matter. If you can target exactly the right people and show them hyperrelevant, customer-centric ads that drive them to hyperrelevant pages on your website, you'll be doing very well. If you remember back to Chapter 2, this is the traffic portion of building linear conversion funnels.

There are lots of people out there buying traffic these days. If you're not optimizing that traffic, you're probably wasting money. There's always a way to get better converting traffic, which usually involves being more targeted and following the principles of HCRO. Look at traffic as one part of the funnel, which plays just as important a role in your CRO process.

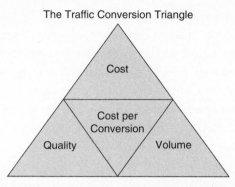

Figure 13.1 Cost, volume, and quality of traffic are all components that affect the cost per conversion, which determines how profitable a specific source of traffic can be. Each of these elements can be manipulated to affect the cost per conversion.

At my company ConversionCore, we have multiple traffic optimization partnerships with PPC-type companies. We optimize using the elements inside the model we developed called The Traffic Conversion Triangle (see Figure 13.1). The center of the triangle is "Cost per Conversion," which is the bottom line for how we evaluate traffic. Cost per conversion is basically asking, "How much money are you paying to get a conversion?" It is affected by three factors—the cost of the traffic, the quality of the traffic, and the volume of traffic you're generating. All three of these elements work together, affecting each other and your overall bottom-line cost per conversion.

The customer-centric mind-set is extremely applicable here. Generally, the more targeted your traffic, the better off you will be. However, sometimes if the traffic cost is low enough, you can get the cost per conversion you need through more volume (not necessarily better targeting).

Over time, each element in the triangle affects the others. For example, the lower your cost, the more volume you can buy. Likewise, the better the quality, the more you'll be willing to pay. There are two other components that are important to mention—time and competitive landscape. Typically, buying traffic is all about the competitive landscape. Popular ad networks, such as Google AdWords, base your cost on many factors, but the competitive landscape plays a big role. The traffic will be more expensive based on how much others are willing to spend on the same traffic you want to buy. Another component is time. The longer you're with a certain ad network and the more you spend, the better deal you'll probably get. This is especially true in AdWords. Also, the longer you run ads on a network, the more data you get about your campaigns and the more wasted expenses you are able to find and eliminate. This improves the quality of the campaign over time. In general, campaigns that run longer and spend more tend to do better. So, when optimizing traffic using the elements in the Traffic Conversion Triangle, remember these other factors can help you, too.

Advertising platforms are constantly evolving, and special software is being developed that gives you the ability to identify individuals, their likes and dislikes, their location, and more. That information gives us the ability not only to make our ads more customer-centric but also to follow that customer-centricity all the way down the linear funnel to the bottom line conversion rate.

Consider this next section an overview of some of the things that can be done to optimize your traffic streams and to develop those linear conversion funnels. There's a lot you can do with optimizing traffic, and traffic is very dependent on your niche. Hopefully, this knowledge will help you find paths you can take to get you where you want to go.

Pay-per-Click (PPC) Traffic

PPC is a form of advertising where you build ad campaigns, and you pay a certain amount of money every time someone clicks on an ad. The most popular form of PPC traffic is called paid search traffic. This is when someone goes to a search engine, such as Google, and the ads show up on the side or top of the results page. The costs are not stationary. PPC is essentially run on a complex auction system where you bid against your competitors for the best traffic. Depending on your industry, you could be paying a few cents per click or in extreme cases even more than $100 per click. Obviously, with that kind of money on the line, you want to optimize your campaigns carefully to keep costs as low as possible. How competitive you can be often comes down to conversion, and ultimately ROI.

Google AdWords is one of the most well-known players in the PPC advertising field, but there are other search engines, including Yahoo! and Bing, which have their own networks. With networks such as AdWords, you have the ability to target the audience, split test the ads, change the cost you're willing to bid for those ad placements, and even customize where the person goes after the click. This functionality makes it much easier to start developing more customer-centric linear conversion funnels.

When you're optimizing traffic for a lower cost per conversion, your campaigns will be continually evolving and improving. For example, in AdWords, there's a term called *click-through rate* (CTR), which is the number of people who click an ad versus the number of people who saw the ad. CTR is an important microconversion point, so you'll want to improve it as best you can. In Perry Marshall's book, *The Ultimate Guide to Google AdWords*, Marshall talks about all sorts of ways to improve your CTRs and design entire campaigns to get better conversions with your AdWords traffic. He also details how to split test your ads and optimize for the lowest cost per conversion. The principles in his book are great examples of ways to optimize your traffic.

Pay-per-View (PPV) Traffic

No, we're not talking about on-demand movies. PPV advertising is where someone searches for something or goes to a certain website, and because the website has special ad software installed, an advertisement pops up in a new browser window (usually behind the current window). Sometimes it's more than just an ad that pops up; your actual website opens in the new browser. Typically, PPV traffic tends to be very cheap (as low as 1 cent per view) because the traffic is not necessarily highly competitive. The viewer wasn't necessarily looking for your website; it's more like an interuption-based ad, like radio or TV, so conversions are typically lower. That's why PPV traffic is much more of a volume game in most cases. Certain networks also give you the ability to target certain keywords as well as specific website URLs, which means when someone visits a certain website, or searches certain terms, your ad displays to the user. This can be an effective way to pull potential customers away from your competitors.

There are lots of PPV networks you can purchase traffic from, including TrafficVance.com, MediaTraffic.com, and LeadImpact.com. Be aware that some PPV networks can have a higher cost of entry, and you may even need an introduction from someone already using the systems.

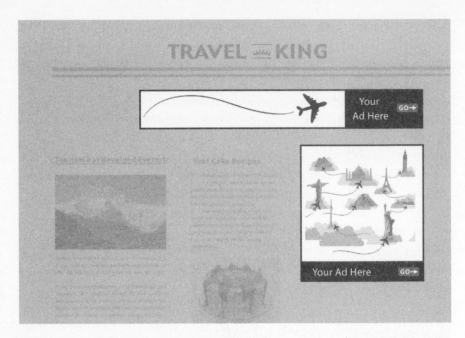

Figure 13.2 Display ads are the ads you may have noticed all over the Internet on sites like NYTimes.com and Yahoo.com. Display networks give you access to push your own ads all over the Internet.

Display Networks

Have you ever been on a website, such as NYTimes.com, and seen a random banner ad on the side or seen blocks of ads that look like Google results pasted onto certain websites? These are both forms of display ads, which are most often managed by a third-party system known as a display network. Any company can get access to many of these networks to push their banner and text ads to websites across the Internet.

When you use the display networks for your campaigns, your ads will show up in a certain box on a website participating in the network (Figure 13.2). You can target general topics, website URLs, and more. Display networks are traditionally less expensive than search traffic because people viewing the ad don't necessarily have an intention to buy at that moment. They are just seeing a passive ad on a page. However, just as with PPV, this is where volume comes into play for getting better conversion rates. Google Display Network (GDN) is one of the largest players in this field, but there are plenty of others, including Advertising.com and Specific Media.

One great way to optimize display networks is to target certain geographical areas. For example, if your best customers live in Houston and you target people who live or work near Houston, you're going to get better-targeted traffic. The rest of the HCRO equation here is to take visitors to a landing page that mentions Houston prominently, and then mention Houston in any follow-up e-mails or phone calls. This is a very basic example of the linear conversion funnel strategy using geotargeting and optimizing lower-quality display network traffic.

Video Advertising

When talking about video advertising online, there are a couple types you can do. One is an extension of the display network advertising, where you're displaying banner or text ads on or around videos in places such as YouTube. The other type is short video commercials that play before, during, or after the main video. The little banner or text ads are overlaid on top of the video as it's playing, so they behave similarly to other display networks. You can buy these ads on YouTube, Vimeo, and other video networks through Google AdWords video campaigns. With these ads, you're able to use contextual targeting based on keywords, and you'll have a lower cost per click than other places online.

There are also commercial video ads, which are more like traditional TV commercials online. These show up before, during, or after a video. You might see a video commercial on YouTube, but you'll also see them on sites such as Hulu, CBS, or even magazine websites such as Forbes.com.

Which one will work best for you is all a matter of accessibility. For example, you can access YouTube through Google AdWords. With Hulu, you can buy the advertising, but the targeting process is left up to them, at least for now. For specific networks, such as CBS, you need to be part of their network of advertisers. Display networks, such as Google, are more accessible than the others. The costs for banner and text ads are much less expensive. Video commercials are more costly, and results depend on your ability to create a high-quality video that engages the viewer. Companies who use video commercials tend to use them the same way as traditional commercials, for branding awareness and conversions rather than to get a click. But that doesn't mean you can't get conversions through video style ads online.

Social Media Advertising

There are hundreds of social media platforms where you can buy advertising. The biggest ones include Facebook, LinkedIn, Pinterest, and Twitter. Each has its own uses, and not every company or product is going to convert well on every platform. We've found the easiest one to access hypertargeted "business to general consumer" traffic with at the moment is Facebook. You can target almost anyone based on all sorts of demographics and psychographics, including age, gender, geographic location, interests, likes, groups they belong to, and a whole lot more.

LinkedIn, on the other hand, is really good for business-to-business (B2B) advertising. For a long time, B2B businesses had trouble marketing online because of what we then called B2B Marketing Disorder. It was really hard to buy traffic on traditional ad networks because it was difficult to determine what keywords high-level decision makers might be searching for. When we did dial in on certain keywords, we often found it wasn't the decision makers searching for products to buy, but rather people simply searching for more information. For example, a medical equipment company might bid on disease-related keywords, but rather than reaching hospital administrators, they reached patients looking for information. This made making good ROI difficult to achieve online.

LinkedIn has done a great job of bringing businesses together in one place, collecting the data, and helping to solve the B2B Marketing Disorder. These days if you sell medical equipment and want to reach hospital administrators, LinkedIn might be perfect for you. It's primarily a business social media platform, and you're able to tightly target people based on business data, such as job titles people have, companies they work at, skills they have, and years of experience. Because LinkedIn lists people's job positions, you can get your ads directly in front of the people you're trying to target, no matter how few of them there are. You can finally be customer-centric when targeting B2B customers.

Real-Time Bidding or Demand-Side Platforms

Real-time bidding (RTB) happens when a platform bids on your behalf in the space of a few milliseconds. For example, if someone visits a travel website, the website pings the various RTB platforms with pertinent data about the visitor. If that person were in your target profile, the platform would send back your bid. Then the website takes all the bids and decides which ad to display. This happens with no visual delay to the visitor.

RTB platforms are becoming popular because they act like a form of artificial intelligence (AI) to combine ad networks and use automation to optimize traffic buying automatically. You can give the platforms all your buying specifications, and they'll find the best ad networks and websites to bid on for you.

Although the platforms' goal is to optimize your traffic for you, we've often found if you have the skill to optimize your own ads, the individual ad networks often give you the features to optimize more and target better. With that said, we have found platforms such as these to be very valuable, for at least data gathering on the networks may have the most potential. They can be used to point you in the right direction toward the right networks and websites to use. Site Scout is one of the better RTB platforms we've had experience with; some others include Jumptap and Right Media.

Organic ("Free") Search Traffic

Organic, or "free," search traffic comes to your website when people search for certain keywords and click on the nonsponsored links on a search engine results page. The term *organic* came from the idea that the more relevant results would naturally move to the top of the results page. The top results were the most relevant to the searcher. Search engine optimization (SEO) is a process that developed around the idea that you could optimize your website to rank higher on the results page for your best converting keywords.

In theory, the higher you rank, the more traffic you get. The SEO industry developed partially because there were no up-front costs associated with it. In the beginning, all search results were organic, and even hobbyists could make serious money if they knew the latest SEO tricks. Over time, the evolution of search engines has made organic traffic much more competitive. Although organic used to be thought of as free traffic, it's become less free because of the competitive nature of the SEO space. Outsourcing SEO has almost become commonplace. Even if you're doing your own SEO, you're still paying for it with your time. The reason organic traffic and SEO is still associated with the word *free* is that once you have your ranking, it's theoretically less expensive to maintain it than with paid traffic. With paid search traffic, you have to keep buying it over and over. The moment you stop, the traffic stops.

One of the other factors to consider with organic search traffic is the quality of the traffic that clicks on organic tends to be much lower. Because the search results are surrounded by paid ads, the people clicking organic results are more often window-shoppers—people who are just looking for information, rather than actual buyers. Once again, every business and market is different. SEO is still a thriving industry, and organic traffic could be good for you if you can keep the costs low and focus on customer-centric targeting. Just don't let your company be sucked into SEO without considering and tracking conversion rates.

Big Data Analysis

You may have heard the buzzword *big data* recently. What this typically refers to is analyzing massive data sets, such as census data, and then looking for patterns in the data that can be used in a variety of different ways. In the case of traffic buying, my company ConversionCore uses big data analysis to become more customer-centric by targeting the right people. In our big data analyses, we typically have access to more than 1,000 points of data on individuals—which can include really insightful items, such as financial stability, heavy transactors, and so on. When you're able to target your traffic with that much data, getting the conversions down the line can become much easier.

At ConversionCore, we also use this concept of big data to optimize our advertising spent in other places, such as display networks. We are able to identify potential opportunities that most competitors miss. It's been really fun for us to see the results we can get from this type of analysis.

Other Sources of Traffic

Buying traffic from networks is all well and good, but it's important to remember there are also other sources of traffic out there. This is another case where every business is different, and you just have to test things out to see what works for you. Here are a few ideas to get you thinking:

- *Off-line Advertising:* Radio, TV, billboards, and print publications can still be great traffic sources for certain industries. They can be risky, though. Be sure to test and track each traffic source, if possible; determine if the ROI is worth it. Taking some cues from the Test Before You Test method could help lower your risks in these areas, if you're just getting started.

- *Affiliate or Joint Venture (JV) Partners:* Sometimes other people with access to your target audience can make great partners. It's common to pay affiliate or JV partners a percentage of your revenue, but you can often come up with other creative ways of compensating people for sharing your message with their lists. The more targeted the list, the more customer-centric you can be.

- *GDN Search Companion:* This is one of newer features that Google AdWords gives you access to. It allows you to market to people who haven't necessarily been to your website but who have searched for certain keywords. Even if they've never interacted with your company at all, you can tag them with a code (cookie) based on their search behavior. Then you can better target your ads to those individuals. This is called *remarketing* and we'll discuss it further in the chapter on follow-up marketing.

Common Mistakes to Avoid with Traffic

- *Don't be oblivious to what traffic you buy and when.* Look at results by geography, time of day, day of the week, season, and so on. What season is that target's area currently in? You may want to advertise differently during Christmas than in the summer. Also, you may not want to advertise with a phone number as the conversion point when no one is there to answer it. If you don't pay attention to time and location factors, you might be wasting money even on the cheaper traffic.

- *Don't skip experimenting with keywords.* Keyword research is free using Google's Keyword Planner. Spend some time researching alternative keywords. Find out what your competition looks like. Split testing your ads, just like split testing your web pages, is a great way to improve them.

- *Don't count on SEO exclusively.* It often takes a lot of effort to get good rankings on search engines, but the results are far from predictable, and can even be volatile at times. All your rankings and hard work can disappear in an instant with one Google update. Just a flip of the switch, and you're back to square one. This can be devastating for a business.

- *Don't bring customers back to the wrong place when remarketing.* A common mistake I've seen in the past is posting a remarketing ad to bring people back to the general website. Bringing them back to the general website would be considered a company-centric ad because it focuses on the brand or company, not the individual. Now, although these ads do convert and do bring people back to the website, it's often much better from a conversion standpoint to design product-specific, or category-specific, promotions, if you can. These display the particular product or category and link back to that product sales page or category page. Don't make them hunt around your website all over again; take them straight there. That is much more likely to convert than just sending them back to your home page. This can be accomplished through a Google AdWords account. Basically, you can set things up on AdWords so that if someone visits a certain page (URL), they are added to a list for that page. Then you can remarket to that list and send them back to the same page.
- *Don't spend time or money on customers who've already purchased the item when remarketing.* Another common mistake to avoid is assuming all the people who come to your website are prospects. I've seen companies waste tens of thousands of dollars remarketing to customers who've already purchased. As we learned in the funnel chapter with concave funnels, it's pretty common to waste money on bad traffic. If you can, it's a good idea to separate these data and cookie customers differently than prospects. You'll have a much more efficient campaign if you focus on prospects.

CHAPTER FOURTEEN

Follow-Up Marketing Strategies

As part of the holistic approach to CRO, it's important to consider how your follow-up marketing affects your Bottom Line Conversion Rate. After all, it may take more than one visit to your website or further education before a prospect is ready to buy. Sometimes it can take months or years of follow-up before they finally convert. There are many techniques for follow-up marketing. In this chapter, we're going to cover two of the most accessible and highly effective follow-up technologies—e-mail marketing and remarketing.

Using E-mail Marketing for Follow-Up

E-mail marketing is one of the most powerful marketing tools for just about any business, whether you sell online or off-line. If you're not familiar with e-mail marketing, the basic concept is that you use e-mail to keep in touch with or market to your prospects and customers. The goal is to eventually convert prospects into customers and keep customers coming back (maybe even bringing some friends). Remember back in Chapter 3 when I said it's important to capture at least an e-mail address? This is the reason why. You're going to use the e-mail addresses you collect to create a list. Then you're going to follow up and create a relationship with each person on your list, hopefully for many years to come (or at least long enough for them to buy your product or service).

A list is just a database, or collection of names and e-mail addresses (and possibly other pieces of information). In more traditional programs, such as Constant Contact, iContact, AWeber, and Vertical Response, most users will only have one list. More advanced users might separate their lists into groups. A group might be as simple as a *customer* or a *prospect*. The idea behind this and the real power comes from list segmentation. When I talk about lists, I'm usually talking about list *segments*. Segmenting your list is one way to make your e-mails more customer-centric and far more effective.

Segmenting Your List

No matter what you sell, you're going to have people on your list who you should talk to differently than other people. Maybe you have some people in the early stages of the sales process and others who are almost ready to buy. You'll want to send e-mails with different content, different tone, and different timing, depending on the person. This is easily accomplished with list segmentation using sophisticated e-mail marketing software, such as Eloqua, ExactTarget, and Infusionsoft.

Usually, you'll segment people into tightly focused lists based on very specific parameters. You can tag them as "prospects from April's seminar" or "stage 3" or "bought product X." You can also tag based on demographics, psychographics, location, and even actions such as attending an event or clicking certain links. The more tags a person has, the more tightly you can target your message.

Once you have a tagging system in place, you can divide your list into more customer-centric sublists on the fly and send targeted e-mails to only the people in a particular sublist. A less sophisticated group might be "customers," but a tightly focused segment would be "customers who attended this year's convention, bought the upgrade package, and filled out a survey about a certain speaker." The e-mail you send to *those* people will be extremely targeted because you know a lot about them. This might sound like a lot of extra work, but the software helps you automate the process relatively easily.

You could see a boost in conversion rates just by the simple act of segmenting your list. However, using CRO with e-mail marketing gets much better the more you focus on the customer and on building an individual a message as possible.

My E-mail Marketing Formula

E-mail marketing is so powerful for conversion purposes because it allows you to establish a relationship and build trust over time almost for free. Although traditional follow-up strategies such as phone calls, in-person visits, and direct mail are very useful, they all have large direct costs associated with them. E-mail probably won't replace these other methods completely in your business, but it does handle much of the follow-up work for minimal cost.

A website can be very impersonal, and it can take some time before people are ready to buy from you. With e-mail marketing, though, you can give them all the time they need—as long as you don't bore them, annoy them too much, or become irrelevant. Relevance is key here. People can unsubscribe at any point, or worse, they can mark you as spam. If you lose them, they probably won't come back.

Some experts say e-mail marketing is dead because people don't like lots of e-mail in their inboxes. But that's just not true. They don't like *irrelevant* or *unsolicited* e-mail. If they sign up for your list, they *want* to hear from you. As long as you keep relevance in the front of your mind when communicating with your list, and you don't overdo it, they will happily read your messages. E-mail is just like any other tool. It's all in how you use it.

Throughout this book we've been talking about ways to make your marketing more customer-centric. In the case of e-mail, everything is based on the right content, the right timing, and the right list (or recipient). If you get these three pieces of the puzzle right, you'll be well on your way to increasing your bottom line conversion rates with e-mail. You'll want to pay close attention to split testing to get these pieces right. Just as we've discussed in other chapters, understanding the Universal

Successful Email Marketing = RC + RT + RL

Figure 14.1 Successful e-mail marketing requires you to get three things right: the content, the timing, and the list segment.

Conversion Logic and psychology behind e-mail marketing will help you more than just memorizing best practices. Every e-mail list is different. So, what do I mean by the *right* content, timing, and list? Let's dig a little deeper into this formula.

- **Choose the right content**. Make sure you are providing value to your list by including relevant, useful, or entertaining information, not just your latest sales pitch. People tire of constant commercials in their inbox and quickly tune you out. It's all about making e-mail marketing part of your linear funnels. Every list is different, so you'll need to figure out what the right balance of information to sales messages is for you. For example, maybe a good balance would be sending two or three informational e-mails for every sales e-mail you send if you need to nurture your prospects a bit. Or maybe your prospects already know a lot about the product, and they just need a good sales e-mail to seal the deal. If you're already segmenting your list tightly, figuring out the right content will probably come more easily.
- **Use the right timing**. You don't want to send too many or too few e-mails to your list, but how do you know what's too many or too few? The right timing is a point between what you need and what they need. Their tolerance for your e-mails is based on the relevance and value you are delivering, and that's tied closely to *when* you decide to send a particular e-mail.

    When we talk about timing, it's important to understand that there are two basic types of e-mail messages: autoresponders and broadcasts. Autoresponders (also known as *sequences or campaigns*) are sent on an automated timing schedule. As soon as someone meets the criteria to receive the message, it goes out. The same sequence is mailed, on the same schedule, no matter when someone is added to that sequence. So Jane might start the sequence in April, and Harry might start it in December. However, they will get the same sequence of messages on their own timeline.

    The second type of message is a broadcast. This e-mail goes out one time, on the exact day you decide. If Harry signs up for the list even five minutes after the broadcast is sent, he will not receive it. He'll have to wait until the next one is scheduled.

    Timing is also about the frequency of your e-mails. There's no such thing as e-mailing too often, as long as you deliver what your list is expecting, or you stay within their tolerance levels. If you tell your subscribers you'll be e-mailing them once a month and you send something every week, people may complain you're spamming them. If you tell them you'll e-mail every day and you send only once a month, people may forget about you or feel like you're not living up to your word. I've done that myself, to be honest. I've gotten busy and forgotten to e-mail often enough.

• **Send to the right list segment.** Your list can be segmented based on the individual e-mail you're sending, which creates a much more customer-centric experience. Sending to the right list is all about defining the right segment. If you have your list divided into big-picture groups, it's going to be more challenging to send a highly relevant e-mail. The more you segment your list, the more relevant the e-mail will be for each individual. Sending irrelevant e-mails to people increases the individual's chance of opting out of your list altogether. Autoresponder sequences can be designed on a per-segment basis, making them tyically more effective in the long run.

When you segment your list tightly, you can create some great opportunities with cross-selling products and services to different groups. If people buy product A, they might also buy product B—but only if you ask them. If they're on a one-size-fits-all customer list, you may not know they haven't yet purchased product B.

Types of E-mail Marketing

Over the years, two primary types of e-mail marketing have evolved: company-centric and customer-centric. In the realm of customer-centric e-mail, other types have evolved, including product-centric, action-centric, and date-centric. Depending on your business, you may need a healthy mix of these to attract, acquire, and maintain your customers. It's important that you know the technology is accessible and often feasible for businesses of all sizes.

Company-centric e-mail is what most people think of when they think of an e-mail newsletter. It's also what everyone thought e-mail marketing was about for years. It's a broadcast e-mail sent on behalf of the company, on the company's schedule, full of generic content written to appeal to a mass audience. With a typical monthly newsletter, a company might deliver some industry tips or an article about what they do. It's sent on their schedule, so if someone signs up a day after the newsletter goes out, they won't get any communication for 29 more days. Basically, they are pooling everyone together because the schedule and content revolves around them.

Customer-centric e-mail, on the other hand, revolves around the individual customer and his or her needs at a particular time. Maybe individuals get a newsletter every two weeks, but it's sent out based on when they signed up. So the timing is different for every person. Every customer gets the same experience. The content also revolves around the individual customer's needs and desires. When you've segmented your list well, you know exactly what to send people because the content is based on what they've said they want in their behavior, not what the company *thinks* they want.

This applies to more than just content and educational sequences, too. Think about your billing e-mails. If you invoice customers on the first of the month, that's company-centric behavior. If you bill customers 30 days after they order, that's customer-centric. Everyone gets the same experience, often based on the day they opted-in.

Product-centric e-mails center on certain products or product lines. They can be sales sequences designed to lead the reader to a sale of the product or ancillary products. Or they might be consumption sequences, where the consumer has already purchased and is being educated on different features of the product and being encouraged to use it regularly. No matter what the desired outcome, these messages are all about a specific product or service. The messages can be stand-alone e-mails, but they tend to be more effective when designed as autoresponder sequences.

Action-centric e-mails are hyperrelevant, customer-centric sequences triggered by a certain action customers or prospects take. When they take an action, such as visiting a web page, buying a product, or clicking a link, they get a sequence based on that particular action. It's no longer just revolving around the customer; it's based on what the customer is doing or already did. For example, you might want to use an action-centric sequence when someone abandons a shopping cart or buys the basic version of a product instead of the premium one. These sequences can be used to educate, entertain, or upsell. Because they are automated, you don't have to think about it once they're set up.

Date-centric e-mails are hyperrelevant, customer-centric messages sent based on what day or time of the year it is. Almost anything can be tied to a date, including birthdays, anniversaries, appointments, holidays, annual seminars and conferences, webinars, events, and even tax deadlines.

Overall, if you want to improve your conversion rates, it's best to get as targeted as you possibly can with your list segments, timing, and content. The more segmented your list is, the more customer-centric you can make your e-mails—right down to the date visitors sign up, the links they click, pages they visit, videos they watch, and all the ways they interact with your company.

Using Dynamic E-mail for Advanced E-mail Marketing

The most successful companies are getting more relevant and more targeted. It's getting to the point where you can send individualized messages in an automated way. An individual e-mail might have five different versions of the same message. A person will receive the best version for him or her based on your testing and segmentation data.

Basically, you're creating custom versions of e-mails to appeal to the right people in the best way. Each person will convert at a different point based on where they are, who they are, and what their intentions are. Wouldn't it be cool if you could send automated e-mails to *individuals* based on what motivates them, drives them, and gets them to convert? You can when you focus your segmenting and split testing tightly.

Just a few years ago, people needed coding specialists to help send dynamic e-mails that really customize themselves to the individual. Tools like Eloqua have recently started making this easier. Even if you don't have the budget to hire coders with this kind of conversion experience, you can get as close as possible on your own using tags and segments.

How do you individualize messages to thousands of people at once? Following are a few ways to think about individualizing messages. Even if the technology is out of reach for you, you should start thinking in these terms and do the best you can in order to get better results.

- *Demographics:* If you ran tests and discovered that pink converts well for women and blue converts well for men for your list, you can change the design, depending on which gender the e-mail is going to, and test your suspicion. (I was purposefully generalizing with this example.)
- *Personality type:* If you know some of your list converts better with short, aggressive messaging (for spontaneous personalities) and another percentage converts better with long-form copy with lots of examples (for methodical personalities), you can choose which copy is displayed to which subscribers.
- *Shopping cart behavior:* You might send a recommended products message to your subscribers based on items they've placed in a shopping cart but then abandoned, or you might base an e-mail on individual items they've placed on a wish list.
- *Website behavior:* If someone visits page 5 and page 10 on your website, and we know people who do that will often buy widget X, then every time someone visits those pages, it could trigger a custom e-mail about that product.
- *Search behavior:* You can keep track of people's keyword searches on your product website and develop profiles for what each person likes. Based on that data, you can customize e-mail messages that market to them according to their keyword preferences. For example, you might give a limited-time discount on a product they were searching for in an e-mail a few days later.
- *Comparison behavior:* If a visitor looks at three different brands of essentially the same product but doesn't buy right away, you can send an e-mail reviewing all three and persuading him or her to purchase the brand with the biggest profit margin. Or you can send a special offer for today only on the product with the biggest margin. It's a special deal that happens to be exactly what they wanted. (What a convenient coincidence!)
- *E-mail ad-libs:* In this form of dynamic e-mail marketing, you might have an e-mail with five different versions of each paragraph in the message. Then according to your customer data, you mix and match the paragraphs (or even individual sentences) to best suit each person. The message is the same, but it's presented in the best way for the individual person. You might use words such as *suck* for one type of person who responds to edgy styles and *disappointing* for another type.

You can also test and track different types of content. Certain subscribers will convert better with images or video; some will prefer written messages. Once you know which version an individual prefers, you can send more of that type of message in the future.

The More You Test, the Better It Gets

Dynamic e-mail marketing is much more than simple segmentation of your list. It's automated segmentation on the fly. Yes, you have to do more work up front. If you do it right, you'll probably know more about your subscribers than they do about themselves. You have to test, test, and test some more. The more data you collect and the more you tailor your marketing to your customers, the better your conversion rates will be. This is why I tell my clients to start collecting all this data now and as they go. Start tagging and identifying everything you can about the people on your list. If you have to start from ground zero when your competition already has lots of data to use, you're going to be way behind. You should also consider list appending using retrievable big data. At ConversionCore, we have seen great things come from combining data.

There's a cool side effect to all this dynamic marketing. From the subscribers' perspective, you are paying special attention to their needs. You're catering to exactly what they want and how they want it. You respect their time and don't waste it with useless e-mail. To them, you're a hero! The happier they are with your company, the more they'll spread the word, which means your lists (and profits) will continue to grow.

How to Split Test E-mail

You already know that split testing involves taking two or more versions of something (such as a web page), splitting the traffic so that some of it goes to each version, and then seeing which version gets a higher conversion rate. You can do the same thing with e-mail. Some e-mail marketing companies even include split testing as a feature of their software.

There are lots of ways to split test e-mails, depending on your goals and what e-mail marketing platform you're using. Assuming you have a good e-mail marketing provider with solid deliverability rates, the first hurdle you have to overcome in e-mail marketing is getting e-mails opened. That's the job of the subject line, so you can split test the same message with different subject lines to see which ones get a higher open rate (Figure 14.2).

For example, do you get more opens with a name in the subject line or no name? Do you get more opens with a teasing headline or a shocking one? Keep track of which subject lines test best so that you can use them again (or imitate the style) in the future. Using strategies like Test Before You Test can help with a shortcut, but only real-life testing is going to give you true results.

Once you have a good open rate, you can test what message components get people to take action. Usually the action is clicking on a link to go back to your website, but it could be other actions, such as calling you, forwarding the e-mail on to a friend, or watching a video. Does your list respond better to a colorful e-mail full of pictures or a plain text e-mail? Do they want long, detailed stories or just a quick introduction and a link? Again, split test the same e-mail written different ways and in different formats, and see which ones get the best response.

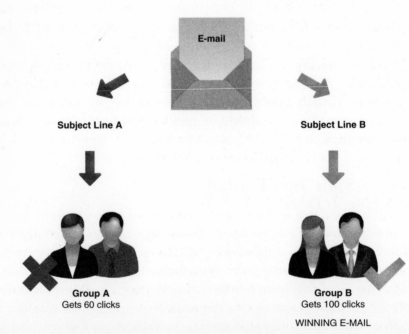

Figure 14.2   It's a good idea to split test your subject lines to increase your open rates, as well as your click-through rates.

Of course, if bottom line sales are the goal, you also want to track which e-mails bring in the most money. It's not always going to be the one with the most clicks if the clicks don't convert further down the line.

Remarketing Strategies

Have you ever been car shopping and found a brand or style you've never heard of before and the next thing you know, you see that car everywhere? It's on every street corner. You see so many people driving around in one, and you could swear you've never seen it before. Suddenly, you see it everywhere.

The psychological name for this is the Baader-Meinhof phenomenon. What you 're suddenly noticing was always there, of course. But now it's in the front of your brain, so you're more aware of it. Remarketing takes that same concept and mimics it on purpose as a marketing tool by *purposefully* recognizing when you look at something and then following you around and projecting it in front of you every now and then. Let's say you went into a Ford dealership, and you saw a special model you liked and were thinking about buying but weren't ready to buy right then. If the dealership paid people to drive that car and follow you around for the next two weeks to remind you about it, that would be remarketing in a nutshell.

It sounds silly, right? Well, actually it would be really cool because it would definitely work on a psychological level, but it's probably way too expensive and not realistic for a car dealership. However, on the Internet, it's not silly at all. It's totally possible and works really well to boost conversion rates. Remarketing is a form of follow-up, so it falls to the right of the Holistic Conversion Timeline.

Here's How It Works

The term *remarketing* literally means "marketing again." A visitor is identified as having been to your website and clicking on your ad, or something like that. That person has been marketed to once and can now be remarketed, using the information we know from the first encounter. Traditionally, this is done with cookie tracking. A cookie is a little bit of code that is automatically embedded in the visitor's computer browser. When a cookie is detected, it sends certain information or instructions to the website you're browsing.

For example, when you go to a website that uses remarketing, the second you land on the website, it embeds a cookie. This cookie lives in your browser, not on the website, so when you leave the website, the cookie is still there in your browser. When you browse around the Internet, the cookie is detected and will automatically launch relevant ads. Basically, once the cookie is in place, it can follow you around the Internet, displaying ads for a certain item you viewed or from a certain brand (see Figure 14.3).

The really cool thing about remarketing is the visitors are still anonymous. In the past, if they didn't identify themselves, there was nothing

Figure 14.3   Remarketing is the process of getting people to return to your website hours, days, or even months after they've left.

much you could do to get them back. With cookies, you can still capture them and follow up with them, even though you don't know who they are yet. It's a way to capture back some of your traffic, even if they aren't ready to be identified yet. With remarketing, you can still access some of those anonymous suspects and prospects, follow them around, and hopefully get them to come back and try again.

Figure 14.3 is an example of external remarketing. The ads are showing up *outside* the original website. Now, you can't just hijack another website, so to speak, with your ads. Instead, you sign up with a remarketing ad network and work through them. A common remarketing ad network people are familiar with is Google's remarketing ad network. If you've ever gone to a website, such as NYTimes.com and all of a sudden you see an ad on the side of the screen for a company or item you've just recently browsed, that's external remarketing. A cookie was put on your computer, and now Google is displaying those ads just for you because they know you were interested. The external website where you're seeing the ad has been compensated in return for that ad space. The longer external remarketing is around, the more people get used to seeing hyperrelevant advertising all the time, which may mean in the future they will be more and more important to your sales funnel.

Internal Remarketing

This is marketing your own products or services on your website in dynamic locations. (Dynamic means they're always changing.) For example, you could have ad spots on the side of the page or a banner at the top of your home page where you display those featured (cookie-connected) products. There are lots of options for how and where you can do this. Even the section of related products in the shopping cart can be considered remarketing if it's dynamically created and connected by cookies.

Let's say someone landed on your product page for tennis shoes. From then on, that user is marked as being interested in your tennis shoes within the browser he or she is using. As this person goes through your website, you can show different advertisements and specials and features of the tennis shoes that were viewed previously. When the person comes back to the website at a later time, even another day, you can even show those tennis shoes on the home page. That's internal remarketing.

Amazon uses internal remarketing all the time. It suggests certain products for you based on something you've already searched for or reminds you about what products you've already viewed.

Common Mistakes to Avoid with E-Mail Marketing

- *Don't be afraid to jump in.* Even if your business is a small business, don't worry that e-mail marketing is beyond your capabilities. It may take a little time to get used to segmenting your list and thinking from a customer-centric point of view, but it's worth it. Tools such as Infusionsoft are priced for small businesses and provide the technology as well as the strategy coaching you can use to implement many of these ideas. These tools can help you get better results.

- *Don't assume you have to buy the data.* When I talk about psychographics and lots of data gathering, people often think they have to buy the data. That's one option, but there are other ways to find things out, as we learned in Chapter 5 on data gathering. Something is better than nothing. Don't feel like you have to know everything about every customer to get started testing.

- *Don't oversell in e-mails.* Remember that with many sales processes, you need to warm visitors up first before they're ready to buy. If you hit them too soon or too hard, you could lose them, or worse, you'll be labeled as spam and it could get harder to e-mail anyone.

- *Don't forget that deliverability is key.* You can't really utilize any of these strategies if your e-mails aren't getting delivered. Beware of what deliverability rates you are getting, as well as the rates your e-mail company gets overall. All the e-mail marketing conversion knowledge in the world is useless if the e-mail never reaches its recipients.

- *Don't annoy people to death.* I see this too often. People send too many e-mails too close together, and it drives people mad. It hurts you rather than helps you. Strive to find the right level of e-mail tolerance from your audience, and remember different segments will have different tolerances. You don't have to send every e-mail to your entire list. That's what segmenting is for.

- *Beware of purchasing e-mail lists.* There are plenty of unscrupulous list brokers that ignore e-mail spamming laws. You want to be careful about how you acquire your list.

- *Don't miss great timing of an event because of a split test.* I see so many larger companies focus too much on split testing, and they miss out on opportunities to contact their list.
- *Don't split your list in split tests carelessly.* If you're split testing without software that does it automatically, be cognizant of how you split your list. You don't want a bunch of the same kind of people to be on one side because then your data will be skewed. It should be as random as possible.
- *Don't forget to be careful with small lists.* If your list is not big enough to split test and get 95 percent or above in statistical significance, find another strategy, such as the Test Before You Test method, to get what you need. Or at least be careful of how you interpret the data that comes back. You may be led to a wrong conclusion, and down a rabbit hole with no exit.
- *Don't stick with just websites for remarketing.* Be creative. Don't let your remarketing efforts stop with just website ads. You can also run remarketing campaigns by e-mail, even direct mail. Because *remarketing* technically means "market again," follow-up e-mail campaigns are technically another form of remarketing. Most marketers think of it as cookie based, but don't let that stop you from reaching out to people in other ways. For example, you can supplement your remarketing cookies with an e-mail campaign. The more ways you can remarket to someone in different targeted, customer-centric ways, the better your conversions will be. In the chapter on e-mail marketing, we're going to go into follow-up marketing by e-mail to boost your efforts.

Build Your Skills

The skills lab for this chapter will help you learn how to segment your list and create more relevant e-mails to boost your conversion rates.

You can find this skills lab at www.ConvertEveryClick.com/chapter14

Hook Me Up, Benji!

Get access to FREE small-business guides and resources from Infusionsoft.

Go to www.ConvertEveryClick.com/hookmeup

CHAPTER FIFTEEN

Advanced Strategies from Benji's Conversion Vault

You don't need to use advanced strategies to benefit from Holistic Conversion Rate Optimization (HCRO). Even if all you do is implement a few of the ideas presented up to now and split test your ideas regularly, you're likely to see improvement in your bottom line conversions.

I do want to share some of my out-of-the-ordinary ideas with you. Normally, these strategies are reserved for my clients and my conversion coaching group. Some of my clients have made millions using these exact strategies. They are powerful ideas, based on sound psychological concepts, but some may seem to contradict what logic tells us is correct until you know the logic behind the curtain. We may *think* people will act a certain way, but in reality they act completely differently, which is why testing is so important. As we discussed in the section on "usability vs. CRO," sometimes conversions increase when you put obstacles in the way, rather than make the path as smooth as possible. Sometimes the perceived value of a product increases when we're forced to wait for it.

These strategies aren't a perfect fit for every business. But they are very creative and fun, and can unlock great gains if implemented correctly. While the strategies I'm sharing here were developed by our team over five years ago, they still deliver breakthrough successes for our clients—right alongside our more recent innovations.

Strategies like the ones I'm about to share are products of innovation and evolution. They are what can happen when you get in the habit of thinking from a conversion perspective. I'm hoping the ideas will ignite a spark in your brain and light up the creative thought process so that you can invent cool and creative ideas to test on your own as well.

If you're skeptical about the results you'll get, I encourage you to give the ideas a try in your niche and test the results. You may be surprised by how people actually behave in certain circumstances.

Advanced Strategies 1–3: Three Ways to Use Animation

Animation, in this case, is anything on a web page that moves. It could be a rotating image slider or a moving progress bar. With web technology, such as JavaScript and HTML5, you can do all kinds of cool animations on your website, including ticking clocks, moving logos, spinners, and loading bars.

Now you may be thinking, *I thought Flash animation on a website was frowned on these days*. You're right. Flash animation is frowned on mainly because of the proprietary, not universally accepted nature of Flash programming, especially on Apple mobile devices. HTML5 is the new standard and has made animation much more commonly accepted.

You don't want to just toss up an animation because it looks cool, though. Every element on your website should have a purpose. There are many ways to use animation to enhance conversions on your website. I'll discuss three ways next.

The Shimmer Effect

The first idea I want to talk about is using animation as a way to draw the eye to a particular spot on the page. I call this particular strategy the Shimmer Effect because you're using a tiny movement to draw the eye to a specific part of the page. It takes only a little bit of movement, a mere shimmer, to attract the eye.

Think about it. If you're looking at a flat screen where nothing is moving and all of a sudden one little thing moves, your eye will immediately go to the thing that's moving. Conversely, if there's lots of motion on the screen, your eye will gloss over or get lost in the chaos. (If you'd like to see a funny illustration of this concept, go to YouTube and search for "Selective Attention Test" by Daniel Simons.)

Imagine you're in the desert. There's nothing around you but sand as far as the eye can see. Suddenly, the sun hits a tiny piece of glass in the sand and it shimmers. That's the effect we're looking for here. If everything on your website is still, a shimmer will attract attention. Let's say you have a landing page, and you want people to fill out an opt-in form. Adding a tiny bit of animation on the form will bring people's attention to it.

Now, you don't want to be obnoxious. Adding flashing arrows or bright lights might diminish your credibility and annoy your visitors. You might have seen those in the early 2000s. Be subtle. All you need is a little shimmer or subtle animation if the rest of the page is still.

Stopping Animations

You can also help direct attention by *stopping* any animation going on at certain times. For example, once people start filling out a form, you don't want them distracted from the job at hand. Anything moving on the page, such as a rotating image slider, is going to distract them from the form. One technique I frequently use is to stop all movement on the page while the person is hovering over or filling out a form. It takes some special coding to manage this, but it shouldn't be expensive.

Using Load Speed Manipulations

Over the years, Google has trained web designers and Internet marketers to load their pages as fast as possible. They reward fast-loading pages with higher search engine ranking, so everyone tries hard to get a near-instant page load speed without realizing this logic can work in the opposite way to your advantage.

In the same way you can use animations to draw attention and exert a little bit of control over visitor interaction with your page, you can also use one of my favorite tools, load speed manipulation. That word *manipulation* may sound sinister, but we're not manipulating the person, only the speed at which certain parts of the page load onto the screen. When you control what loads when, you influence what the visitor pays attention to most.

Now, I don't want you to think that a slow page load will help conversions. It probably won't. But with a skilled use of JavaScript, you can purposefully manipulate a page so that certain sections of the page load sooner than other sections. Say you have a landing page, and you want people to focus on the web form more than the written content. If you make the form load a tiny bit faster so that it's the first thing people see, they may naturally give it more attention. Or it may test better as the last thing they see, so it's the last thing their eyes land on. Maybe you want people to watch a video before they start reading through a long portion of text.

This all happens within milliseconds of entering a web page, so users rarely even realize there's a delay. However, the psychological effect is still there because the subconscious brain sorts through things faster than our conscious brain registers anything is going on. When you use this technique, you have a small piece of control over the visitor's subconscious mind and eye. You're telling it where to look and in what order to look at objects.

I've actually used the examples I described here multiple times in many variations. In all cases, we saw a conversion increase of more than 30 percent, so you can imagine how excited they were to use this technique on every web page they created. Again, this technique takes a skilled coder on your team, and you must choose the correct order and timing. If executed incorrectly, you could affect your page negatively. Testing is critical here. But the results can be spectacular and it's well worth investing in top talent to get the coding done right.

Advanced Strategy 4: Using Instant Chat and Instigated (Proactive) Chat

The more people get used to communicating instantly through text message, instant message, and other chat-style interfaces, the more this technique will be used as a regular feature online. Depending on your business model and audience, adding a chat function to your website now could be a really smart move.

There are two different kinds of chat functions. Instant chat is a chat feature that sits on your website all the time so that your visitors have a way to contact you without having to pick up the phone and exit the web experience. The visitor starts the conversation. This version of chat can help almost any website because it gives the visitors a feeling that they're not alone. Help is just a click away.

The other kind, instigated chat, is when something your visitors do (or don't do) automatically triggers a chat box to appear. Maybe they've been on the page for a certain amount of time, and a chat box pops up with a friendly message, such as, "Do you have a question? Click here to talk with a support agent now." Sometimes instigated chat is triggered automatically for all visitors; sometimes it only pops up if people start filling out a form and try to leave or if they hover over a certain part of the page.

Having instigated chat on your website can be a positive or negative thing, depending on your business model. If you have a business-to-business product line or a highly technical product line, it can be very helpful. Some of the early adopters of this technology were custom computer-type service providers and other highly technical businesses. Chat allows the visitors to ask questions and get answers in real time, while they are still on your website. This can be a huge help in reducing shopping cart abandonment (see Figure 15.1).

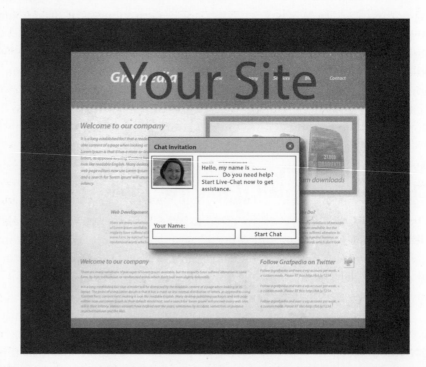

Figure 15.1 Instigated chat is where you start the conversation with the prospect, instead of the other way around. It can be very valuable, especially for technical products or services where the prospect could be more likely to buy if they were able to interact with an agent easily.

On the other hand, you don't want your chat feature to feel like a pushy salesperson following your visitor around the website. That might hurt your conversion rates. Using the customer-centric mind-set, try to get inside the visitor's head and figure out if he or she has any burning questions that need to be answered right away. Does the visitor need to make many choices to complete the order? Do people tend to land on an action page, but don't buy? Do people feel the need to ask questions about your product or service before they buy? Is your pricing competitive? Are your packages confusing? If the answer is yes to any of these, then chances are chat could be a good investment for you.

Assuming you have someone online available to speak with visitors at any time, instigated chat can be very effective. A common mistake to avoid here is thinking any traditional phone salesperson can handle chat questions. You may want someone familiar with the product who can answer questions and make a subtle call to action without annoying the visitor. Selling on the phone is different from written sales, and both are different from chat sales. You read people differently in chat; it's a whole different type of communication. Often someone who enjoys social media interaction on Facebook or Twitter may be a better person to convert sales on your chat interface than people who are better at communicating over the phone. If you don't have the right team, there's nothing wrong with asking someone if you can call them and requesting their number after they are engaged.

Getting chat right can take a little bit of trial and error. You don't want to give up too quickly. It can take a few months to get your team oriented on how to communicate better through chat before you start to see the results. Once the results come in, they can be very encouraging. I've personally seen extremely high increases in conversions and customer satisfaction just by engaging the customer through chat and instigated chat methods.

Advanced Strategy 5: The Foot in the Door Technique

I named this after a strategy used by door-to-door salespeople. Long before the advent of the Internet, one of the only ways to sell to people was to go door to door. Salespeople would literally put their foot in the door to force people to listen longer to the sales pitch. They couldn't close the door in the salesperson's face, which meant the salesperson just bought himself or herself a little bit of time. The psychology behind this can be applied online. Obviously, I can't put my foot in the door physically, but using the same psychology online, I can buy myself some time to explain the benefits of whatever product I'm selling. This technique online essentially makes people wait but uses animation to keep them from getting frustrated and leaving.

In a recent example, I used this technique with a client who had a product that people bought quickly, used right away, and then never looked at it again. It had a fairly low perceived value and price to match. We needed to convince visitors that the value was higher than they perceived it to be and keep them in the funnel long enough to purchase the product from us and not a competitor. So, rather than removing obstacles and making the sales process faster and smoother, we put obstacles in the way. We made people wait.

There are many ways to use this strategy. In this case it was as simple as adding an extra step in the funnel. For this client, we added a "loading" screen with a progress bar and slides that changed every few seconds as the progress bar ticked along (see Figure 15.2). Each slide included different benefits and features of the product. While they were

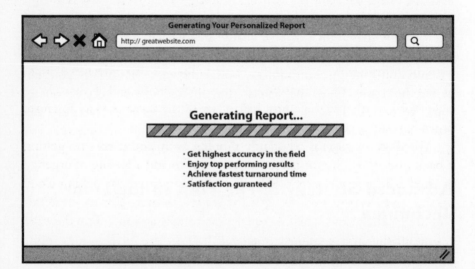

Figure 15.2 Sometimes slowing down a process can raise perceived value and can have a positive effect on conversion rates. Put your digital foot in the door by using this old principle and adapting it for online use.

waiting, visitors were being educated on the value of the product. We asked people to wait several minutes before completing their purchase. This loading step also helped increase the perceived value because the delay was seen as an investment of their time. People's subconscious minds don't want to waste all that time by clicking away to another competitor.

There are two different psychological factors at work here. Putting your foot in the door gives you more time to sell the product. In addition to that, the fact that we made them wait turned a quick purchase into an investment process. Why would they want to go back and start over with a competitor now?

The Foot in the Door technique is a great example of how to use psychology and old-school off-line sales tactics to get a point across or create a higher perceived value. We've used this technique many times, and while it works only for certain situations, it doesn't work in all cases. You really have to test it carefully, but when it works, it's amazing. Recently, we were able to get a 363 percent increase in conversions on an already relatively high-converting website using this technique.

Advanced Strategy 6: Creating Urgency with Countdown Timers

Almost anyone experienced in sales will tell you urgency is a very useful ingredient for closing a sale. It can force people to make decisions more quickly and will often boost sales. This works really well online, especially with a little psychological help. One of my favorite ways to create urgency is using countdown or expiration timers.

We all know time is constantly slipping away, and there's no getting it back under any circumstances. If you want to add a feeling of urgency, or even a little anxiety, try adding a countdown timer or ticking clock on the page. Make sure you say what it's for, though. The clock represents how much time is left for the person to take action before the page expires or the offer is no longer valid.

This works best for short periods of time, such as minutes. It can work the other way, too, but just be careful that you don't create the opposite effect by making them feel like they have plenty of time and can make a decision later.

As with many other conversion strategies, some companies use this strategy effectively, but they do it originally for reasons other than conversion. It just happens to help with conversion, too. Ticketmaster uses this idea really well to sell concert tickets on their website. In order to buy the tickets, you must complete several forms, including credit card information. On every page where you have to fill out a form, there's a countdown timer. You have 10 minutes to fill out one form, 6 minutes to fill out the next one, and so on. It's very obvious what you're expected to do and that you don't have much time to do it. One of the reasons Ticketmaster is so successful with this tactic is it makes total sense. Concert tickets can be highly sought after, and if one person ties up a whole block of tickets for hours at a time, it's not fair to everyone else who wants to buy them. So Ticketmaster has a perfectly legitimate reason why it can allow you only a small window of time to complete the transaction.

Advanced Strategy 7: Discount Remarketing

A more advanced strategy we've tested successfully over the years with clients is discount remarketing. Others do not do it very often—yet—but it's a very high-converting strategy for certain offerings.

If someone comes to your website and doesn't buy within 24 hours, the assumption is that person isn't going to buy. We can use remarketing to bring this customer back. But bringing such people back can be a waste of time and money (especially if it's a short-term product) because if they didn't buy the first time, they probably won't buy the second time. They need an additional incentive. So it's more effective to let the remarketing ads offer something like a special Blue Sale of 20 to 40 percent off. You're literally offering a discount on the same product viewed 24 hours earlier, but the sale is good for only a day or two at most.

If you have the ability to post the sale website-wide, you can really go all out. However, you can still use this strategy with something as simple as a banner on your home page. The key is that the sale is good only for the person who's looking at it, even though it seems like a sale for everyone. The only time the discount message appears is when the website detects a particular cookie. This is a customer-centric way of presenting a formerly company-centric discount strategy. This discount concept can be used in lots of creative ways, but the basic concept is very sound and has converted very well in almost every situation we've ever tested.

Advanced Strategy 8: The Smooth Capture Methodology

I'm glad you're still with me because I've saved the best strategy for last. It's called the Smooth Capture Methodology, and it's one of my favorite conversion tools. I've been using it now for over five years on many websites, and it's useful on almost every website out there, especially landing pages and even shopping cart websites.

Smooth Capture is the psychology of creating a highly effective web form process, both for the user and the company. It solves many problems for prospects, including:

- They don't want to spend a long time on a form.
- They don't like changing pages (as with multistep forms).
- They don't like feeling overwhelmed by long capture forms.
- They perceive their time as limited and are more and more impatient these days.

Think about how you feel when you're faced with filling out a long web form, and by *long*, I mean more than six fields or so (as we discussed in Chapter 3). It's overwhelming, isn't it? Some forms can get so long that no matter how badly you want to buy the product or get the information, it's just not worth the time and effort to fill out all those fields. With this technique, you can get away with asking more questions with less risk of them abandoning the form. Smooth capture overcomes that overwhelmed feeling and enables you to gather more information from the visitor in a comfortable, inviting way. It also ensures that if the visitor is unable to complete the form, you can often follow up with them later due to a key feature of smooth capture.

Smooth capture is an advanced method of creating multistep forms. It is not a short capture or a long capture, nor a short-to-long capture. Compared to all of those types, I have found smooth capture to be exponentially better for conversions in many different scenarios.

How the Smooth Capture Methodology Works

1. Visitors never leave the page as they move from step to step in the form. Nothing changes on the screen except the fields in the form. Traditionally, we've accomplished this through JavaScript.

2. Added animation between steps creates a smooth, consistent, noninvasive feel to the transition process. Instead of feeling like a second step, it feels like a continuation of the same process. It keeps the user's brain from resetting the way it would if the screens were moving from one step to another in a traditional multistep form. As each new step is loading, you may want to include an animated spinner to indicate the form is being processed. When people click Next or Submit and nothing happens, they often start wondering if they've done something wrong. You don't want them second-guessing anything, so show them the information was accepted and is being processed. If it's built well, it should load for less than a second, anyway.

   Recently, I've seen this strategy being used in mobile apps to transition from screen to screen. It works on a small mobile screen for the same reasons it works on a web form. Essentially, smooth capture is becoming a usability norm for mobile, although I can't take credit for that natural evolution.

3. The form has fewer than six fields in each step. Step 1 might have two fields, step 2 might have five fields, and step 3 might have three or four. It's a good idea to vary the number of fields in each step so that people don't expect the same number each time.

4. On step 1, you may or may not want to overtly indicate there are more steps. This might seem annoying, but in reality and in tests, people breeze past that thought because of the smooth animated transition between steps. They often don't even realize that what's happening is not typical because the usability is so natural feeling.

5. On subsequent steps, you provide some sort of clue as to how far along they've gotten. If there are only two steps, you can simply say "Last step" on step 2. But if there are three or more, at some point you should give them a clue how much farther they have to go using step indicators as we discussed with multistep forms. You can use an animated progress bar or a simple label that says "step 2 of 3." This lets them know they don't have much more to do; there are

only a couple of fields remaining, so they think to themselves, *I may as well just keep going.*

6. On the final step, there should be a label that says "Last step" or "Final step." Psychologically, visitors are thinking they've come all this way; they might as well just finish the last screen so as not to waste all that effort.

7. Psychologically speaking, there are two ways you can ask for information in your web form. You can ask for the most important contact information, such as name and e-mail, first. This assures you will get the most critical information up front.

   The other way to structure your fields is to ask some of the more basic, nonidentifying questions first to get them invested in the process. Then ask for identifying information at the end. This comes from the psychology of survey writing, where they save the more difficult or personal questions at the end. The goal is to increase your bottom line conversion rates, so test each way to see which one is more beneficial to your business.

8. Send the information to your database upon submission of each step so that even if visitors abandon the form before the end, you can still follow up with them later by e-mail or phone. This is probably the least common and largest reason smooth capture is so effective. While most people think about the microconversion of the lead, because of our holistic approach to CRO, we know that the Bottom Line Conversion Rates go up significantly with this strategy when coupled with follow-up marketing.

Smooth Capture is extremely powerful, but it does have a lot of moving pieces that need to be designed, coded, and planned out correctly. You should definitely split test your forms. It makes me a little nervous to mention it, but I've never seen this technique fail when implemented properly and tested against any other kind of traditional web form, including short capture, long capture, and even multistep forms. But just so you know I'm not blowing smoke, we have real data to prove it. If Smooth Capture is not working for you, there's probably something that needs to be adjusted or fixed with the implementation.

CONCLUSION

The world is changing. You now have the ability to learn more and more about individuals and cater to their needs and wants. As time goes on, everything around us will become more and more customer-centric. Whether you're a small-business owner or work for a Fortune 100 corporation, you and your company can benefit from using Holistic Conversion Rate Optimization strategies to get as close as you can to converting every click. If you don't move with the world and start using the tools available to target individuals and split test your ideas, you will fall behind all the other companies that do. It's less about using the data and systems and more about innovating *how* you use them. The most successful companies will focus in on their targets and build marketing around the individual.

I hope you see by now that conversion rate optimization is far more than simply tweaking and testing web pages. It's all about crafting holistic marketing around the customer. The customer-centric web strives to cater to every individual as much as possible. Creating your sales funnels, web pages, e-mail, and all your marketing with the individual customer in mind first is the best way to increase your conversion rates. Just in case I haven't said it enough, no matter what you do, always be sure to split test and use your data wisely.

What Should You Do Next?

You may be wondering, What are the next steps? How do you put these techniques into action? I've created the skills labs specifically to help you gain a deeper understanding of certain techniques. You can access them by signing up for your free account on www.ConvertEveryClick .com/skillslab.

You can also get more in-depth, focused conversion help with your business by joining Benji's Conversion Mastermind coaching group. Find out more about this personalized approach to learning Holistic Conversion Rate Optimization at www.ConvertEveryClick.com/mastermind.

Hook Me Up, Benji!

Head over to www.ConvertEveryClick.com/hookmeup for access to all the free bonus resources mentioned throughout the book.

FREE Wistia account
    —Video hosting with great analytics
FREE 30-day trial of Optimizely
    —My favorite A/B split testing tool
FREE 30-day trial of Visual Website Optimizer
    —Another great split testing tool
FREE 30-day trial of Crazy Egg
    —For heat map analysis and data gathering
FREE ClickTale account
    —Another great tool for heat maps and data gathering
FREE 30-day trial of jiveSYSTEMS
    —Video e-mail and marketing tool
FREE Small Business Success Guides from Infusionsoft
    —For small business marketing automation, e-mail market-
      ing, and more.

SUPER CHARGE YOUR BUSINESS WITH CONVERSION-CENTRIC WEB SERVICES

ConversionCore: Holistic Conversion Rate Optimization Consulting

We help medium-to-large sized companies improve their Bottom Line Conversion Rates based on their overall marketing and sales strategies. We offer both consulting-based and done-for-you services.

ConversionCore.com/ConvertEveryClick

ClickCore: Conversion-Centric Web Development

We design websites that integrate the entire marketing and sales strategy from the traffic stage through follow-up. Each design process begins with a consultation with a ConversionCore strategist. It's a holistic approach that combines smooth funnel plans and attractive design to reach maximum ROI.

ClickCore.com/ConvertEveryClick

Have Benji Speak at Your Company or Next Event

Benji's extensive experience in all aspects of Internet sales and marketing processes means he has unique insight into what makes businesses work online.

His regular speaking topics include:

- How to grow your business exponentially using Holistic Conversion Rate Optimization techniques.
- How to create more freedom in your business by building automated systems that handle repetitive tasks without you.
- How to harness the entrepreneurial spirit and use that energy to create an inspiring business, even if you're starting from scratch.

BenjiRabhan.com/Speak

INDEX